T0106281

ELIZE HATTIN

The Naked Truth

about

you

Your Path to an Extraordinary Life Revealed

BALBOA.
PRESS

A DIVISION OF HAY HOUSE

Copyright © 2011 Nuntio Pty. Ltd.

All rights reserved. No part of this book may be used or reproduced by any means, graphic, electronic, or mechanical, including photocopying, recording, taping or by any information storage retrieval system without the written permission of the publisher except in the case of brief quotations embodied in critical articles and reviews.

Book cover, concept design, illustration and layout by: www.soulspace.com.au
Editing: Wendy Smith, jewelsee.com.au

Balboa Press books may be ordered through booksellers or by contacting:

Balboa Press
A Division of Hay House
1663 Liberty Drive
Bloomington, IN 47403
www.balboapress.com.au
1-(877) 407-4847

ISBN: 978-1-4525-0282-3 (sc)
ISBN: 978-1-4525-0284-7 (hc)
ISBN: 978-1-4525-0283-0 (e)

Library of Congress Control Number: 2011918353

Because of the dynamic nature of the Internet, any web addresses or links contained in this book may have changed since publication and may no longer be valid. The views expressed in this work are solely those of the author and do not necessarily reflect the views of the publisher, and the publisher hereby disclaims any responsibility for them.

The author of this book does not dispense medical advice or prescribe the use of any technique as a form of treatment for physical, emotional, or medical problems without the advice of a physician, either directly or indirectly. The intent of the author is only to offer information of a general nature to help you in your quest for emotional and spiritual well-being. In the event you use any of the information in this book for yourself, which is your constitutional right, the author and the publisher assume no responsibility for your actions.

Any people depicted in stock imagery provided by Thinkstock are models, and such images are being used for illustrative purposes only.
Certain stock imagery © Thinkstock.

Printed in the United States of America

Balboa Press rev. date: 11/28/2011

To my amazing husband Wald for your
unfailing support.

To my gorgeous girls, Evah and Eden for your
wordless inspiration.

To my wonderful parents Andries and Louise
for your encouragement and help.

Preface

This book was born out of my sincere desire to help people. As a life, business and executive coach, it is my privilege and honour to speak with different people daily and assist them in creating their own unique extraordinary life. Every day I meet people who want their lives to matter, who are doing the best they can with what they know and who want the world to be somehow different because they are alive. Every day I see people who love their kids and families and who strive to find a work life balance. Every day I meet with people who are determined to step up and overcome the challenges that come their way. Every day I speak with people who want the rest of their lives to be the best of their lives. Every day I wish that there were more hours in the day to speak with more people, to assist more people on their journey, to help more people live extraordinarily. That is why you are holding this book in your hand. I wanted to speak with you and assist you and now I can!

The information contained in this book was born out of my own desire to understand what life is about. Ever since I can remember I have had a deep desire for wisdom and understanding. I enjoy working things out, piecing different bits of information together to form a coherent whole. I am driven to know and understand in a logical and systematic manner. The information in this book is the result of many years of reading, researching, questioning, studying and working with clients. But mostly the information in this book is the result of praying and seeking God's wisdom and understanding.

In my quest to produce a book of excellence, I needed a LOT of help. I would like to thank Derek O'Connell, Vanessa Chapman, Richard Morris and Rebekah Strachan for their involvement in the creation of The Naked Truth about YOU. I also extend a BIG THANK YOU to my family for their patience, help and support during the writing process. Another thank you to all my clients, you know who you are. Thank you for allowing me to contribute to your lives and in return for contributing to my life in many ways. I appreciate and salute you all!

Deciding on the title was one of the most challenging aspects of this process. I must acknowledge my darling brother Justus Pienaar for his suggestion that contributed significantly to the final title. I would also like to thank and acknowledge all who were present when we decided on the final title, Justus Pienaar, Michelle Pienaar, Maria Prinsloo, Andries Pienaar, Louise Pienaar and Wald Hattingh. Thanks guys!

Now it is my privilege and honour to share my work with you. You are holding in your hand a comprehensive, detailed, logical, proven and fun guide to being extraordinary and living extraordinarily. The program outlined has been tried and tested many times and it works! It has been designed to do more than just inform; please allow it to transform you and your life. I hope that you will engage with this book, complete the suggested exercises and come back to it as a reference when needed. When you do, this program will also work for you!

Contents

CHAPTER 1
You Live in Two Worlds 1

CHAPTER 2
Know Who You Are 9

CHAPTER 3
Understand your Brain 17

CHAPTER 4
Know your Conscious Mind 25

CHAPTER 5
Take Control of Your Subconscious Mind 39

CHAPTER 6
Understand the Basics of Emotions 53

CHAPTER 7
Feel Good! 69

CHAPTER 8
Gain Advantage from Unpleasant Emotional Experiences 85

CHAPTER 9
Smash Your Shackles 105

CHAPTER 10
Master Your Body 111

CHAPTER 11
Live Your Unique Extraordinary Life 123

CHAPTER 12
Make the Most of Time 137

CHAPTER 13
Engage in Your Life's Work 149

CHAPTER 14

Face the Big Four: Change, Problems, Goals and
Others' Opinions of You! **161**

CHAPTER 15

Accept You Are a Spiritual Being **179**

CHAPTER 16

People – How to Predict Behaviour **185**

CHAPTER 17

Be The Best You **201**

Quick reference guide **205**

Biography **207**

Bibliography **208**

Contact details **209**

CHAPTER 1

You Live in Two Worlds

The truth?

What is the truth?
In this post-modern world,
many will argue that the
'truth' is nothing more than a
subjective personal opinion.
There is, however, one
indisputable truth: YOU EXIST.
At this point in time, the one
thing you can know for certain
is: you exist as you are.

Exactly what that means might not be so clear. Your life and existence might often feel like a mystery, even a random occurrence. Do you feel you are merely going through the motions of life? That you are not living, only existing? That life is hard and often meaningless?

You may hear people speak of your authentic self. So who is that person and where do you find the authentic bit? Do you think that you have lost yourself, or that maybe you never quite found out who you are in the first place?

This book will reveal the naked truth about who you are! It will uncover the real deal, no frills, no fuss. This book will lay bare the secrets that will allow you to transform yourself and your life. Exposing the truth might confront you as well as comfort you; and ultimately it will transform you. When you apply the techniques found in this book, your life will become the birthplace for the BEST you!

Where is everything you have always wanted?

We reside in countries with higher living standards and greater opportunities to own, learn, do and experience anything we could ever dream of. Yet most people, even those successful and wealthy by worldly standards, often feel desperate, depressed, stressed, anxious and lonely. Even though our environment contains everything we could ever want or could achieve, we are generally unhappy and dissatisfied with life. As Mother Teresa stated, "The spiritual poverty of the Western World is much greater than the physical poverty of our people. You in the West have millions of people who suffer such terrible loneliness and emptiness."

It seems absurd that people are unhappy when they have every desire within grasp. Our environment has so much to offer. Opportunity abounds: food, drink, telephones, modern housing, entertainment, computers, vehicles, infrastructure, medicine and so much more. Why then do we seem dissatisfied and desperate with our lives and circumstances?

The naked truth is that while our environment is so abundant with opportunity, we are so lacking on the inside. Nothing that you have been striving for or pursuing in your environment has the ability to create a lasting extraordinary life.

No feelings of happiness, safety, wealth and love are hidden in your environment; nothing that you acquire or achieve will bring you lasting happiness, safety, wealth and love. You will never find these feelings in your environment. Happiness, safety, wealth and love and all the other wonderful things you desire are only available for YOU to create on the inside.

You live in two worlds

You live in two worlds. Every day of your life is spent living simultaneously in these two separate and yet connected worlds. They are known as your Inner-world and your Outer-world.

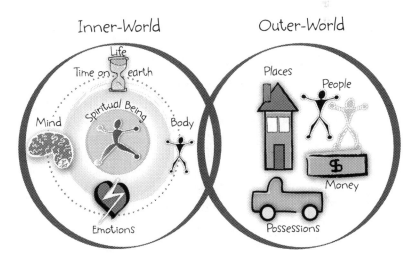

Your **Inner-world** is everything that happens 'inside' you and your body. It includes your spirit, your mind, your emotions and your body. The interactions of these Inner-world ingredients shape your Inner-world experiences.

Your **Outer-world** on the other hand, is everything that exists around you. It includes everything and everybody external to your body. Not only does it include the environment but the places, objects, possessions and people that you interact with daily.

Your Inner-world and Outer-world are interconnected

As you live in these two worlds simultaneously, your Inner and Outer-worlds are connected and relate to each other daily.

How does your Outer-world influence your Inner-world?

As you move through your life and your environment, you encounter different people, places, situations, relationships, etc. All of these elements are external to your body so they form part of your Outer-world.

Your Outer-world influence is two fold:

1. The default position is for most people to allow the environment to profoundly affect their thoughts, emotions and body. The Outer-world has the power to enter and shape your Inner-world and your experience of life as a result.

2. You will also form an interpretation of the people, places, situations and events from your Outer-world in your Inner-world. Your experience of your Outer-world events occurs in your Inner-world. This experience (your thoughts, corresponding emotions or feelings as well as your physiological bodily responses) is based on your interpretation of your Outer-world.

As you will discover later in this book, your interpretation is unlikely to be the 'truth'. Interpretation equates to perception (a function of your mind) of Outer-world happenings. Perception does not allow you to see, feel, hear and interpret your Outer-world accurately.

The substance and strength of your Inner-world ingredients very much determines your interpretation of your Outer-world, thereby determining the quality of your life.

How does your Inner-world produce your Outer-world?

80% of your current life is the result of all the thoughts, emotions, feelings, decisions, choices and actions you have or have not taken over the years. The life you are currently living is the result of your ability to overcome your challenges, navigate your relationships, make profitable decisions, discipline yourself, influence others and know what you want from life. These Inner-world elements have shaped and produced "your" version of the Outer-world.

Therefore, 80% of your Outer-world is a reflection of all that has occurred in your Inner-world. The substance and strength of your Inner-world ingredients determine in the quality of your Outer-world throughout your lifetime.

Take a moment and look around you. Do you feel good about what you have created? Is there any room for improvement?

Which world contains the majority of the challenges you face?

Do you feel that the majority of your challenges are contained in your environment or Outer-world? Do you feel that the challenges you face are things outside of your control? Are they caused by someone or something else? You may be pointing the finger at your parents, partner, boss or even the country's economy. Do you feel you are the victim of your Outer-world, where you are powerless to change things that are less than perfect in your life?

The naked truth is that 80% of the challenges you face are contained in your Inner-world. It is only when you overcome your Inner-world challenges that your Outer-world challenges will be resolved.

This is best explained with an example: Let's assume you face a challenge in your environment, say a relationship problem. You may think and feel that the majority of this relationship challenge is contained in your Outer-world, with the other person and your shared environment.

However, 80% of this challenge was created in your Inner-world. It started with your decision to enter into the relationship and/or shared environment, compounded by your consequent communication, expectations, your reasoning and your emotional reactions.

When you distance yourself from the situation you will see that 80% of the solution to this problem is also found in the Inner-world. Solving this problem therefore entails overcoming the negative emotions that are preventing you from seeking a solution and taking positive action. In order to do so, you will need to face up to your problems and recognise the feelings and thoughts they produce. These negative thoughts and unpleasant emotions are preventing you from making a clear plan for getting out of this problem – a problem caused by your Inner-world.

The fact that the majority of your challenges are contained in your Inner-world is actually great news because while you can only influence the things in your Outer-world, YOU possess the ability to fully control your Inner-world.

This book will empower you to take back control of your Inner-world - your spirit, mind, emotions and body. You will uncover who you really are and how to use your mind, emotions and body to set yourself up for success and to create an extraordinary life by creating an extraordinary Inner-world.

Where is everything you have always wanted?

The greatest myth of our time is that an extraordinary life can be found or created in your Outer-world. An extraordinary life is not something that you can find in your Outer-world like an item waiting for you to buy at the local supermarket.

Other people do not hold the key to your extraordinary life either. The joy of extraordinary happiness is only available in the Inner-world and something only you can choose. Contrary to popular belief, other people or having a partner cannot make you happy. Nobody can guarantee your happiness but YOU.

Money does not guarantee an extraordinary life either. While money can provide a comfortable, luxurious and beautiful environment, it certainly does not guarantee that your life will be extraordinary. Your attitude towards money and the feelings you have about money are contained in your Inner-world.

Your ability to experience an extraordinary life is neither created by nor constrained by money, possessions, titles or other people. Everything you have ever wanted is available in your Inner-world.

Ultimately you are the only person in control of your Inner-world. There are many people and forces beyond your control in the Outer-world, but everything you have ever wanted is available to you in your Inner-world. You can create happiness, safety, wealthy living and love in your Inner-world - you are the only person who can do it for you.

So what is the Naked Truth?

Did you know that YOU have a momentous opportunity available to live the life of your dreams – an extraordinary life of significance, meaning and contribution? But there is a catch! To take advantage of it, you must gain full mastery over your inner self - your mind, your body and your emotions. And that is the only way!

So there it is in a nutshell.

This really is a wonderful opportunity for you but it may also be challenging. Why? Because you will need to make changes to gain full mastery over your inner self. Everyone does! By way of explanation, most of the issues you confront will be inside you, which means that while people may be able to help you, no one else can actually do this for you. As challenging as it might seem, for things to change, first YOU must. That is the naked truth!

This book is designed to help you in your journey. It requires that you learn what you need to know to turn your opportunity into reality. This book will reveal, in a no-nonsense way, how you can live a truly significant life. It will become the manual for your life.

Through your use of this book you will come to realise the naked truth about yourself and even meet the real you. You will learn how you interrelate with the world around you and dig deep to disclose the key relationship between your mind, body and emotions.

Your brain will become more accessible to you and the remarkable power of both your conscious and subconscious mind will be revealed. You will learn about your emotions, the importance of feeling good and that not feeling good can be your prompt for self development. In the process, you will free yourself of the shackles that constantly hold you back.

You will learn to master your body, obtain control of your mind and emotions, optimise your time and engage in your life's work, in order to live the truly extraordinary life of contribution that is before you. You will become a person who benefits from change, finds solutions, sets goals and positively uses the opinions of others as a catalyst for growth.

You will learn both how to create powerful and lasting relationships with the people in your life and how to grow to spiritual maturity. At that point your life will be both extraordinary and powerful, just as you have always wanted.

I sincerely hope you will allow this book to do more than merely inform you like so many other books have done in the past. It is my sincere desire that the naked truths you uncover will transform your Inner-world, creating an extraordinary life from the inside out.

CHAPTER 2

Know Who You Are

Which ingredients
do you require to live
an extraordinary life?

Your extraordinary life starts by creating, nurturing and nourishing an extraordinary Inner-world. This begins with you transforming yourself into being and feeling extraordinary on the inside. An extraordinary life starts with the elements or ingredients that constitute who you are.

Are you aware that you are a wonderfully unique, complex, amazing being? You are more multifaceted, intricate and wonderfully created than you realise. However, this incredible complexity leaves most people feeling confused, baffled and even sometimes bewildered. Most people know more about the garden variety snail than they know about themselves. What an opportunity!

How can you control, manage, or master something you do not understand? How can you create an extraordinary life from the inside out without knowledge of your Inner-world ingredients? How can you gain optimum benefit from anything you do not fully comprehend? Without studying your mobile phone's instruction manual, you would be unable to take advantage of the features it offers. You might be able to make phone calls, but you certainly will not benefit from all its features. The same principle applies to you. Without gaining insight into who you are, you are unable to take full advantage of your features and will never gain optimum benefit from your outstanding complexity. What a shame!

Poor self-knowledge leaves most people feeling powerless, helpless and at the mercy of their Outer-world and circumstances. How can you master life if you cannot make sense of it all? How can you live extraordinarily if you feel powerless? How are you expected to forge and maintain loving relationships with others if you cannot figure out who you are, never mind understanding your partner, friend or sibling? It is impossible to be the powerful YOU if you are not familiar with your own ingredients, capabilities, resources and potential.

Your Inner-world ingredients: who are YOU?

YOU are a spiritual being having a human experience. Yes, let this truth and realisation sink in for a moment.

YOU are a spiritual being… living as a human being… engaged in a human experience… but YOU are a spiritual being!

You are more than your physical form and human existence. Even though you dwell in the physical world, within a physical form, you are in essence an amazing Spiritual Being.

You are a Spiritual Being having a human experience

YOU, as a Spiritual Being, have been granted a precious gift and three astonishing tools. What gift? What tools? You might ask!

Spiritual Being

What is your most precious gift?

YOU, as a Spiritual Being, have been given a most precious gift - your life. Your life is defined as 'Time on Earth' and is measured by the amount of time you will spend on earth in your human form. Your life, in your human form, has a specific beginning and a specific end. Your time on earth began at the moment of your conception and will end on the day of your human death.

YOU have only one opportunity to live your life on earth. YOU will only receive this precious gift once. Therefore, it is vitally important to fully engage with your life. There will be no second chances; this is your first and final opportunity to experience life as a human being, in human form. So make the most of it; your time on earth is limited! Treat your time on earth as a prized possession. After all, it is a valuable and irreplaceable gift; once the time is spent, it can never be regained.

Is there more to YOU than your mortal frame?

Understand this: when your time on earth ends with the death of your human form, YOU will continue to exist as a Spiritual Being. YOU are infinite and immortal. Even now, YOU will have a deep awareness of your eternal existence. As a Spiritual Being, YOU are timeless and not bound by the human understanding of the concept of time. YOU, as a Spiritual Being, will exist for eternity.

But don't forget, you are only given one opportunity in your human form to live this life - to spend time as a human being - so make the best use of your time!

What tools do YOU have to build an extraordinary life?

YOU have been given three astonishing tools to enable YOU to engage in and with your human experience and your life on earth. They assist you to exist as a human being and are essential for you to be able to use your gift of life. Your tools are:

✓   Your Mind.

✓   Your Emotions.

✓   Your Body.

Residing in your human body is YOU, the immortal Spiritual Being. You are not your mind, or your emotions or your body. YOU are a spiritual being, having a human experience! Your mind, emotions and body are the tools that enable you to navigate through your gift of life.

Sadly, many people do not understand that the mind, body and emotions are tools to be studied, utilised, and mastered. These tools are not who YOU are, nor should you live at their mercy. Rather, YOU, as a spiritual being, must develop and grow in strength, learning to master your mind, emotions and body thus gaining maximum benefit from your astounding tools and living an extraordinary life.

Is your body the real YOU?

YOU are not your body. Your body is the vehicle bearing your spiritual form. YOU are, in fact, a Spiritual Being, which exists in spirit separate from your body. Therefore, YOU do not need your physical body to exist; YOU only need your body to be able to have a "human or physical experience".

Is your mind the real YOU?

Additionally, YOU are not your mind. Your mind enables YOU, as a Spiritual Being, to function as a human in physical form and to live the life YOU have received. YOU have been given the ability to master and control your mind.

Are your emotions the real YOU?

YOU are not your emotions. Your emotions are the link between your mind and body. However, these emotions are incredibly important, as emotions drive actions and actions determine results. Therefore, learning to control and master your emotions will ensure an outstanding quality and experience of life and ensure the results of your life are extraordinary.

Throughout your time on earth, YOU as a Spiritual Being must grow in strength and maturity. YOU can live extraordinarily when you understand the full potential of your astonishing tools (mind, emotions and body).

YOU can and should take full advantage of every feature these tools have to offer. YOU were destined to live a great and happy life. This extraordinary life is now within your grasp, and it is easier to achieve than you might think. Living extraordinarily will be much more enjoyable and fun! You will be more successful, happier and your relationships with others will improve significantly. You and your life will be improved in every way!

The question is HOW? How can YOU take advantage of your Inner-world ingredients; your mind, emotions and body? How do YOU master these astonishing tools? How can YOU take full advantage of your time on earth? How can YOU make your life on earth count? How can YOU achieve your destiny of a great life? Where is the instruction manual for your life?

THIS IS IT! This book is your manual! It will step YOU through a simple, fascinating and ultimately life-changing journey. This book will speak about your mind, emotions, body, life, and spirit, and how they interact with and affect each other. YOU will be amazed at the features of the amazing tools you have been given and how YOU can benefit from using them effectively. It will practically and powerfully demonstrate what YOU are capable of, and what YOU can do to ensure YOU achieve your extraordinary life. By reading this book, you are taking the first step to living the extraordinary life YOU were destined to live!

CHAPTER 3

Understand your Brain

Your brain is a very powerful tool

Observing the complexity surrounding your brain, you realise it is a phenomenal architectural wonderment.

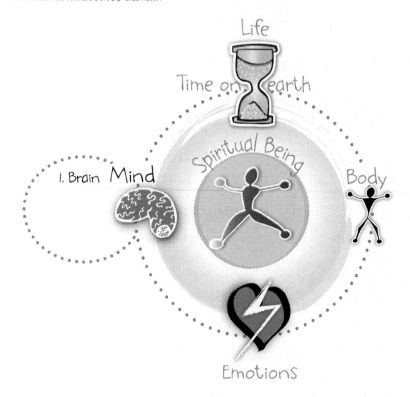

This one organ provides you with the ability to walk, talk, judge distances, move your hands, breathe, blink your eyes, smell the flowers, see the colours of the rainbow, control your heart rate and perform a myriad of other functions in a fraction of a second, all at once!

How complex is that! Plus, the bonus is that it is yours. You possess this wonderfully complex organ inside of you; it is yours to utilise in everyday life and yet, most people do not understand how to operate this tool to its greatest potential. It's the same as driving a car. You can simply drive from A to B, or if you explore the car's greater potential you can learn to operate it in a manner that gives you greater fuel economy, less wear and tear, or even enable the family to experience a safer and more comfortable ride.

It is the same for the human mind. The human mind is one of the most amazing and useful tools in your arsenal, but unless you know how to master your mind and utilise its functions correctly, you will never fully appreciate or benefit from its potential.

YOU are not your mind

Your mind was given to YOU as a tool to utilise in the best possible way. YOU are not your mind or your thoughts. The mind is a tool or instrument which YOU, as a Spiritual Being, use in the physical world to live and accomplish your life's ambitions. YOU have been given your mind as an assignment to master, which cannot be achieved unless you understand what it does and how it operates.

As I have stated before, YOU are not your mind; YOU are not your thoughts; YOU are also not the results of those thoughts. YOU (Spiritual Being) have the ability and the responsibility to master and control your mind. In doing so, YOU will have the resources to achieve your full potential and contribute to the world and other human beings in a powerful way.

In order to fully appreciate your mind as a tool to master, it is essential you understand how it functions. Understanding the mind is the first step to mastering it. So, here is a brief tour of the mind, revealing how it works and how YOU, as a Spiritual Being, can use your mind to live an extraordinary life.

The language of your mind...

The mind's ability to process language is more than just processing the words you speak and hear. The mind has the ability to detect and decipher pictures, sounds, feelings, tastes, smells and words. It can single out the things that give you pleasure, as well as those which make you cringe with distaste. Your mind's ability to decipher all of these is due to the complex structures found within the brain.

Your Brain

The brain itself is made up of a series of structures of cells, hormones and chemicals. While this information may not be new, it is essential to possess a level of understanding of how the brain works in order to master its potential. All of the brain structures work together in unison to ensure your brain functions correctly as a finely-tuned and well-oiled machine.

However this machine needs connections, in this case, millions of connections to allow you to control your body, remember information and enable you to function in your day-to-day life. The most wonderful and amazing aspect of the human brain is its ability to learn, and YOU have the ability to train and retrain it where necessary. You have the ability to form new connections that will enable you to achieve the best possible results.

The best way to understand the connections your mind makes is to understand each component of the brain and how they interact collectively.

Your Brain – How it works? What it does? Why it matters?

Central Nervous System

The brain forms part of the Central Nervous System and, together with the spinal cord, forms the "control centre", coordinating every aspect of your body's daily functions. However, this is not all that makes up your brain. Three layers of membranes called the meninges, cover the brain and the spinal cord. Between two of these layers, the subarachnoid space, the cerebrospinal fluid (CFS) is contained.

Different types of Brain Cells

Did you know you were born with about 40 billion individual nerve cells, known as neurons, within the brain? Unlike other cells within the body, these cannot be replaced if damaged. This makes the cells within your brain highly specialised and fragile and totally dependent on you to keep them healthy. Once they are lost, they will never be replaced.

Your brain cells communicate with each other. No, they don't go out and have coffee every Tuesday, but they do communicate by sending electric or nerve impulses through a system of nerve pathways or networks. These nerve cells are held in place and supported by Glial cells, which also incorporate Astrocytes, Oligodendrocytes and Ependymal cells.

The brain itself is divided into three distinct parts and each part has its own specialised role to play in your existence. First is the Cerebrum or forebrain, the largest component of the brain where most of your higher mental functioning occurs, such as thinking and memory.

The cerebrum is divided into two hemispheres: the right and the left. Ironically, the left side of the cerebrum controls the right side of the body and vice versa. These sections of your brain are easily distinguishable, with a bundle of fibres called the corpus callosum connecting the two halves. Have you ever heard the saying, "When I am not in my right mind, my left mind gets pretty crowded"? This is actually true.

Each hemisphere of the cerebrum is then divided up into four lobes known as the frontal, parietal, temporal and occipital lobes, which individually and/or in cooperation with other lobes control a range of motions and actions throughout your body. However this is not all; the brain also includes the Cerebellum located at the back of the brain, which is responsible for all of the automatic functions of the body. Just think, every time you walk, run, jump, lift your arm or hold a pen, your body is performing tasks subconsciously.

Located at the base of the brain, connecting the cerebral hemispheres to the spinal cord, is the brain stem. It is responsible for every breath, heartbeat, variation of blood pressure and eye movement your body makes. These are just a few areas of the brain's structure; the other remaining areas and their functions are listed below:

Area of the Brain	Function	Description
Cerebral Cortex	Thought Voluntary Movement Language Reasoning Perception	"Cortex" is derived from the Latin word for "bark" because the cortex is the outer layer of the brain. The left and right sides of the cortex are connected by a group of nerves called the 'corpus callosum'.
Cerebellum	Movement Balance Posture	"Cerebellum" comes from the Latin word for "little brain" and is located behind the brain stem. It is in some ways very similar to the cerebral cortex.
Brain Stem	Breathing Heart Rate Blood Pressure	Located between the thalamus and the spinal cordites, it is responsible for all of the basic functions for life – breathing, heart rate, etc.

Area of the Brain	Function	Description
Hypothalamus	Body Temperature Emotions Hunger Thirst Circadian Rhythms (Sleep Patterns)	Only the size of a pea and located at the base of the brain, this is responsible for regulating body temperature and other vital functions.
Thalamus	Sensory Processing Movement	Receives sensory information and relays this to the cerebral cortex and other areas of the brain.
Limbic Systems	Emotions Memory	Responsible for the emotional responses to a particular situation. Also important for memory.
Hippocampus	Learning Memory	A part of the limbic system, responsible for memory and learning.
Basal Ganglia	Movement	Important for all of the body's coordination.
Midbrain	Vision Audition Eye Movement Body Movement	Consists of the superior and inferior colliculi and red nucleus.

Apart from the central nervous system, your body also has a peripheral nervous system, made up of all the nerves that lie outside the brain and spinal cord. The peripheral nervous system, as the name suggests, extends to the periphery or extremities of your body and is vitally important to how your body acts and reacts to the situations surrounding you. The peripheral nervous system can be divided into separate functions:

1. Sensory (Afferent) – allows information to be carried INTO the Central Nervous System (CNS) from your sensory organs, or motor neurons (efferent) which allow information to be carried away from the central nervous system (for muscle control).

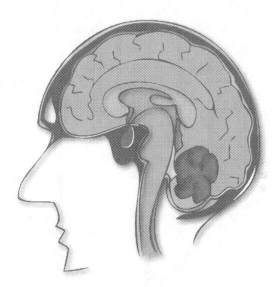

2. Somatic – connects your skin and muscles with the Central Nervous System, or the Visceral nerves which connect your internal organs with the Central Nervous system.

Scientists are still studying, researching and making new discoveries about the brain every day. Your brain is truly an amazing organ, an essential instrument given to YOU to master and use during your life on earth.

Brain versus Mind

While your brain is the actual physical structure, the organ located in your skull, the term 'mind' refers to the functions and tasks your brain performs. A computer analogy explains this well. You can compare your brain to the hardware of a computer, while your mind can be likened to the software, programs and functioning of a computer. So your brain is the organ while your mind is the functions and tasks produced by your brain.

Understanding the functioning of your mind offers you an awareness that will empower and enable you to start the process of mastering your mind.

In the next two chapters, you will learn how the functions of the brain are carried out in your life. This understanding will enable you to discover the secret to how your mind works and how to gain full benefit from it.

CHAPTER 4

Know your Conscious Mind

The brain is a highly complex organ and you are only just starting to understand its intricate workings.

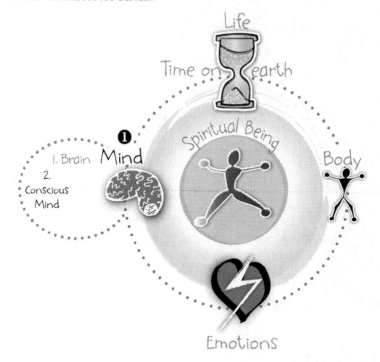

Your brain, as discussed in the previous chapter, is the physical organ responsible for much of your functioning. Each specialised area of this amazing structure could not work optimally without the other; their interactions are infinite and help regulate the human vessel you inhabit.

Your mind depicts the functioning of your brain, effecting how it works in your daily life. The mind consists of two sections, the conscious mind and the subconscious mind. The conscious mind describes the part of your mind of which you are aware, while the subconscious mind is everything that happens in your mind of which you have no awareness. Knowledge and understanding of your mind will unlock the secrets to who you are, why you behave the way you do and what you can do to be the powerful and best YOU.

YOU are not your mind. YOU are also not your thinking. If your mind is currently filled with negativity and self-defeating thoughts and words, YOU are not negative or self-defeating. YOU are a spiritual being who is starting to learn how to take control of your mind and how to master it. By taking control of your mind and your thinking, YOU are taking the first steps towards being the powerful YOU and living your extraordinary life.

Do you Mind? Conscious versus Subconscious

What percentage of your behaviour and functioning is controlled by your conscious mind?

Your conscious mind is only responsible for 6% of your behaviour and functioning. It is a sobering thought to know that you are only aware of 6% of what you do and how you do it. The remaining 94% of your functioning and behaviour is controlled by your subconscious mind. This means you are not consciously aware of most of your daily behaviour and are merely going through the motions, guided and controlled by your subconscious mind.

For example, as I type these words, my mind automatically guides my fingers to the correct keys on the keyboard. I am subconsciously guided through this movement, as my conscious mind is focussed on the next word in the sentence. By investing time to gain the knowledge and understanding of how your mind works, you will be able to control and use your mind wisely. So, let's work with your conscious mind first, as this is what you have immediate control over.

What should you know about your Conscious mind?

Your conscious mind is the "thinking" part of your mind. It refers to the part of your mind that controls everything you are consciously aware of, in terms of your functioning and behaviour. This includes basic decision making, such as choosing when and where to eat, what to wear on a cold day, where to go for the weekend, as well as more complex thinking.

YOU have the ability to control your mind

Greater awareness of how your mind operates will give you the ability to master, control and manage your conscious mind to gain maximum benefit from it. Only when you acquire this new awareness, will you be able to apply your conscious mind to engage more actively in your life.

Six Functions of your Conscious Mind

Bob Proctor teaches that your conscious mind is responsible for six intellectual functions. These functions describe the marvellous abilities and explain the daily activities of your conscious mind. The six functions of your conscious mind are: reasoning, imagination, perception, will, intuition and memory.

Like any organ within your body, the mind needs to be exercised, but it is not as simple as just heading to the gym and giving it a good cardio workout! Your mind needs stimulation and, as the saying goes, "If you don't use it, you lose it!"

Each and every day you condition your mind by repeating certain acts and thinking certain thoughts, thus strengthening and reinforcing the specific connections that allowed you to perform a particular behaviour - just like a good workout! For example, as you repeat or practice certain things, like remembering a specific fact, thinking in a specific way, doing a certain calculation or jumping over a fence, your mind strengthens the connecting wires that already exist for you to behave in this way.

In order to take full advantage of your mind, you must understand, use and develop each of the functions of your conscious mind, conditioning your brain to reinforce these important connections. Most people do not take advantage of all of the functions of their conscious mind and therefore struggle to achieve their best life. Each function offers a precious jewel and opportunity from which you can benefit. Mastering these functions is an essential step in using your mind effectively because each function is a key element for unlocking your full potential. Embrace each function, use each function and enjoy challenging your mind, giving it a good workout and getting the best out of your remarkable tool.

The following section describes all you need to know about your conscious mind; giving you the opportunity to examine it and look for the opportunities to strengthen and utilise every function available to you. Mastering these six functions is the foundation for mastering your mind.

1. Reasoning

Reasoning refers to your ability to think, rationalise and make day-to-day decisions. It reminds you to wear your tennis shoes and tennis clothes when you are heading off for a game of tennis, take a coat on a cold day or an umbrella when it is raining. Reasoning refers to your awareness of your surroundings and your day-to-day thinking.

In his book *The Seven Habits of Highly Effective People*, Stephen Covey states an important principle: Everything is created twice! There are two creations for everything; the first creation and the second creation.

Picture this: you have been asked to build a shed for the back yard. What would you do first? To begin, you would design the shed in your mind, determining what it would look like. You would consider the purpose of the shed, how big it would be and where it would go. This process is known as the process of reasoning – you would reason or think your way through this project.

Once you have designed the shed in your mind and possibly transferred the design to paper, you would go ahead and build the shed. First, the shed was created in your mind, the first creation, using reasoning to design the most suitable shed. Then, you will create it in reality, the second creation. The shed you create in reality is the product of your thoughts and reasoning about it in the first place. You first create something in the mind using reason before you create it in reality.

What happens, however, if you built this shed and it is not exactly what you wanted? You would rethink the design to find a different solution to your current problem. After rethinking the design you would modify the shed accordingly.

Every day you are creating the results of your life through your thoughts and actions. At this very moment, you are in part the product of all the thinking you have done in the past.

What if you do not like the current results in your life? How do you change the results? In the same way as you would reconsider and rethink the shed design, you need to rethink and challenge your thoughts if you are not satisfied with the results you are achieving in your life. First, you must look inwards to your thoughts and reasoning. This process involves examining and questioning your thoughts, challenging the way you think, the assumptions you make and the logic you apply. One of the easiest ways to challenge your thoughts is by asking yourself different questions. Four useful questions to ask yourself in any situation are:

What is good about this? How could I approach this differently? How am I contributing to this situation (good or bad)? When I change my approach, how will the situation change?

YOU are not your thoughts. Your thoughts are a function of your conscious mind. YOU, as a Spiritual Being, have the ability to be aware of and control your thoughts. What would you be thinking if you were setting yourself up to succeed in life? Your reasoning skills can help you train your thinking so that only positive, encouraging, productive and optimistic thoughts are present, dismissing any negative and destructive thoughts from taking over. Challenging and questioning your thinking will enable YOU to take charge of your thoughts, reasoning with yourself to find the most productive manner of thinking. An essential step towards mastering your mind is learning to control it to think the thoughts that will allow you to achieve the results you desire in your life.

2. Imagination

Your imagination is your mind's playing field - it is your ability to see, feel and hear different situations in your mind. It is your natural ability to construct different scenarios in your mind and experience these as if they were real. The word 'imagination' also refers to your capacity to visualise, to see things in your mind or with your mind's eye. Your imagination is your chance to experience different places, meet different people and live a life very different from your own without leaving your chair.

Let's do a little experiment: Imagine you are about to speak at a conference. An audience of 10,000 people is waiting to hear you speak. You are standing on the stage, gazing at the back of the stage curtain that is about to open. You hear the murmuring of the crowd. You feel your paper notes between your fingers. You hear your name and introduction. You are about to face the sea of faces and address the audience...

What did you feel as you imagined this scene? Did you feel excited? Nervous? Anxious? A sense of anticipation? Whatever the feeling, the point is that your body could not distinguish between what you imagined and what was real. Your body's responses and reactions are the same regardless of whether the situation was created in your imagination or in real life. Responses and reactions evoked by your imagination may not be as intense as in real life but they are nevertheless the same.

As we discovered with reasoning, everything is created in the mind first. Your imagination is your key in doing so. It truly is a gift to behold and, if you use your imagination well, you have the ability to travel anywhere, do anything and have anything you wish for. Your imagination gives you the power to experience different lifestyles and worlds, all without spending any money or even leaving the comfort of your own home. Your imagination also offers the opportunity to prepare for any situation before entering into it in real life, making the situation familiar and well rehearsed. Whether it is a job interview, first date, difficult conversation or public speaking, your imagination can assist you to be prepared and at your best.

Remember, your imagination is the key to your creativity and problem solving and your direct link to the world of possibilities…

3. Perception

Perception is a term used to describe the method in which your conscious mind processes, filters and organises information gathered from the Outer-world into something meaningful that you can make sense of. Your mind cannot deal with the multitude of information vying for your attention at all times, so perception sorts the information into something meaningful for you. Neuro Linguistic Programming (NLP), created by Richard Bandler and John Grinder in 1973, offers useful insight into how perception works. Essentially, perception is a three-step process:

Step 1 – The conscious mind takes in information from the world around us. The information is gathered via your senses by using your eyes to see; your ears to hear; your nose to smell; your tongue to taste and your body to feel. The brain takes in thousands of responses from all around your body, compiling them into a sequence that your conscious mind can understand.

In gathering information from the environment, you predominately use three senses over the other two. The three you rely on most heavily are sight, hearing and touch (feeling or experiencing). However, even though you use all five senses, you have a preference. In fact, everyone has a sequence of senses they prefer to use and rely on repeatedly to gather information from their environment. For example, you may predominantly rely on your sight first, then hearing and touch or feeling last. Or you may rely on touch or feeling first, sight second and hearing least; or hearing first, touch second and sight last.

You will not absorb all of the available information from your environment as you will not utilise all of your senses equally. Due to this fact, if there are 100 units of information available in your environment, you might only absorb 70 units.

For example, if two people standing side by side witness an accident, the two individuals will not gather the same information from the environment even though they both experienced the same occurrences. This is because it is highly likely that each will rely more heavily on different senses.

Remember – you do not see with your eyes, you see through your eyes with your mind.

Step 2 – The brain then takes the information it has received and determines if the image presented is familiar and whether it fits with what you believe about the world. You will only see the evidence of what you already believe, that which fits with your programs and beliefs. The filtered out, discarded information is then dropped into the subconscious mind where it is stored.

Therefore, you do not see everything there is to see; you only see the evidence of what you already believe. How you experience the world is based on the substance and quality of your Inner-world. You don't see, feel, or hear the Outer-world as it is; you see, feel and hear the world as you are.

The problem with perception is that you will constantly filter out valuable opportunities for you to be the powerful YOU and live well. If you focus on the negative things you will not notice all the great things in your life and in the world; you will only see, feel and hear more negativity. When you focus on what you want, your perception will show you the opportunities that will allow you to work towards achieving the life you want. Ask yourself each day, "What is it that I am not seeing, feeling or hearing?" and take notice of your environment.

Step 3 – The remaining information is then processed by the mind. This can occur in one of three ways or a combination of two or more. Your mind deletes, distorts or generalises the information gathered while processing it. Sometimes you will use all three, but will invariably have a preferred method of processing which you will use more often than not.

If you favour deleting, you will have the ability to disregard or ignore information quite effectively and will more than likely be able to endure physical discomfort and cope by simply deleting the associated information.

If you happen to favour distorting information during the third step of processing, you will ultimately warp or change the information. For example, have you ever experienced a disagreement where someone says, "That's not what I said!

This is what I said...."? This shows your interpretation of what was said does not match what was actually said. You have changed, warped or distorted the information during the process.

Finally, if your preferred manner of processing is generalisation, you end up creating rules as to how the world operates. These rules will make you feel and be perceived as confident. You feel as though you understand the world and how it works.

The most important thing to realise about perception is that after the filtering process, only some of the information first received remains in your mind. Therefore, it stands to reason that objective reality does exist, but it is near impossible for anyone to see it. The term, "objective reality" refers to the concept that there is a true or real world outside of us which is ostensibly different to the world that we understand. This is because of the unique way in which we each receive information, filter it and process it in our conscious mind. Each of these steps has the effect of changing the reality in some way, to the point where only some of the information first received in your conscious mind remains intact.

Therefore, while it stands to reason that objective reality does exist, it is nearly impossible for anyone to see it. It is there and it does feel tangible to you but you cannot truly understand it because of the way the three-step perception process changes it.

Despite each person's perception of a situation being unique and different, it is very interesting to note that people are generally still able to coherently relate to each other.

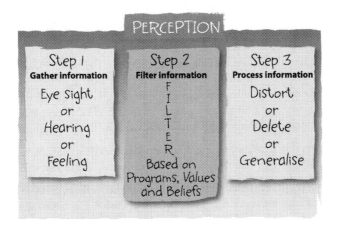

4. Will

Have you ever had one of those days where you felt like you shouldn't have gotten out of bed in the morning and you achieved nothing all day because everything seemed to go wrong?

We have all had days like that, but something kept us going; something kept us in the thick of things, making sure we got through the day. That was your will; it is your mental toughness, it keeps you together when things look bleak.

Imagine yourself as a marathon runner. The first hour or so is easy, just working your way to the front of the pack, settling in for the duration, keeping a steady pace. Then something goes wrong. You take a step just a little too close to a rock and roll your ankle. The pain shoots up your leg; your ankle throbs to the same beat of your heart. You don't think you can make it to the finish line, but you have to, you want to. So much is riding on this and you can almost taste the finish line! As much as it hurts and no matter how much giving up seems to be an easier option, you don't. You stick with it and you make it!

Your 'will' helped you accomplish this. It was there cheering you on, giving you the strength to finish the race even though everything seemed to be against you. In the same way, your will is available to you in your everyday life. The strength of your will at this moment is directly influencing the outcomes you are achieving in your life and how well you are living it.

As a child, you might have been trained not to be strong willed, trained to let go of what you thought, felt and wanted, in order to conform to those around you. However, as an adult, it is essential you regain a strong will, as the strength of your will greatly influences and determines the outcomes you achieve. Fortunately, will is like a muscle, the more you use it, the stronger it gets. Your ability to endure, persist and overcome resistance from yourself and your environment is determined by the strength of your will.

The strength of your will can vary greatly in different aspects of your life. Take Pete for example. Pete discovered through coaching that even though he is very strong willed professionally and in his career, he is weaker willed in terms of his health. He does not apply the strength of his will to ensure he eats a healthy diet and exercises regularly, causing him to be overweight and un-healthy. However, he had no conscious awareness of this because 94% of his behaviour is subconscious. What Pete had to do was apply his conscious mind to all aspects of his life, examining whether he was utilising his will in the necessary aspects of his life.

Take a look at your own will. Is there something that needs to be strengthened? Is there a specific aspect of your life to which you are not applying your will? Alternatively, are you being strong willed in the wrong areas of your life, thus distracting you from being your best and living well?

Will is like a muscle – it needs to be stretched, exercised, massaged – and just like a muscle, the more you use it the stronger it will be and the more easily you will be able to cope with tough or stressful situations. Remember though, as a Spiritual Being, it is still up to YOU to control your conscious mind and determine how and when to apply your will. There will be times when you may just have to walk away, as some battles are just not worth fighting, but then there are times when it is necessary to fight to the bitter end.

5. Intuition

Have you ever felt like you should have turned right at the roundabout instead of left, knowing the traffic jam you are stuck in could have been avoided? Well, that was your intuition speaking to you. It was presenting you with unseen information, seeking to guide you onto a better path. When everything seems equal, your intuition will lead you to the right decision.

Intuition is an awesomely powerful tool! It can pick up on 'vibrations' or intangible data in your environment and guide you to make the right decision. Although often described as a 'gut feeling', it doesn't necessarily originate in your 'gut'. This bodily feeling can be felt in your throat, chest or stomach area.

Did you know that the most successful people often analyse information and make a final judgment based on their 'gut' feelings? A well-developed intuition will enable you to choose the right option or course of action when the way forward is not clearly defined. Additionally, your intuition will let you know when you are in danger.

The best way to develop your intuition is to pay attention to what your body is telling you. This will allow you to understand what your 'gut' is trying to communicate. Furthermore, you need to slow down your thinking. Today's society runs at such a fast pace that it is easy to miss even the most important signals; so slow down and allow your mind to take things in. Finally, you need to become more aware of what's happening inside yourself rather than what is going on outside.

6. Memory

Memory is your ability to recall information. The brain relies on pathways created in the mind in order to remember certain information. The information it recalls could be anything from the name of your grade three teacher to what you had for dinner last Friday night. However, memories fade and details become sketchy and the next thing you know you have lost your car keys!

Just like your will, your memory also needs exercise. Your brain needs to be strengthened and trained and, through repetition, your brain can reinforce existing connections as well as create new, productive connections or pathways. By keeping your mind active, you will boost your memory. You have a responsibility to keep your memory strong, so try a little Memory Boot Camp and keep your memory strong and lean!

Minding your most valuable resources

Additionally, your conscious mind holds two of your most valuable and scarce resources: your attention and focus. There is a limit to what you can give your attention to at any given moment - you are also limited in your capacity to focus. Most people find it impossible to hold two opposing thoughts in their minds simultaneously. Therefore, your attention and focus are incredibly valuable as they are truly limited. Take care how you use and apply these two resources and be disciplined in what you use your attention and focus for, being mindful of their value and importance. Give your attention to that which enables you to be the best YOU; focus on what makes you feel good and that which promotes an extraordinary life.

Being familiar with your own conscious mind and understanding your own reasoning, imagination, perception, will, intuition and memory is the foundation to controlling and utilising your mind to its greatest potential. Challenge your mind and take control of your thinking. Apply your attention and focus to what is wholesome and productive. Your mind is your most amazing tool, so become the best and powerful YOU by mastering it.

CHAPTER 5

Take Control of Your Subconscious Mind

Your conscious mind has a limited capacity. There are limits to what you can give your attention, think about, remember to do and have awareness of in any given moment.

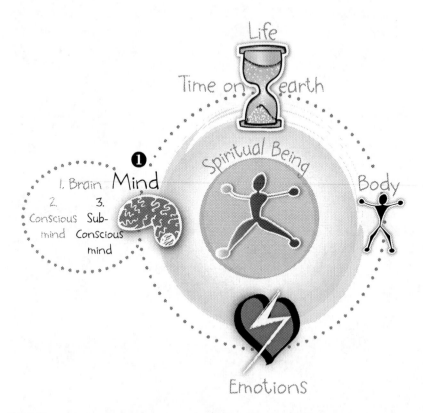

Even if you are as smart as Einstein, the capacity of your conscious mind remains limited. You would not be able to survive if you had to remember to breathe, make your heart beat, etc. as well as walk, talk, work and live life. As you move through life, there will always be enormous amounts of information vying for your attention. If your existence was left solely to your conscious mind, you would struggle to survive. Thankfully, your survival and functioning is not threatened by the limited capacity of your conscious mind. Your mind has something running in the background, much like a power station, that does not require any conscious attention. This is known as the subconscious mind.

We have already determined that your subconscious mind controls up to 94% of your behaviour and functioning. This indicates that 94% of everything you do is being performed behind the scenes without your knowledge, allowing you the freedom to focus your attention on what is occurring in your life.

The subconscious mind, while keeping to the shadows, wields tremendous power, governing the way you behave on a daily basis. Your subconscious mind is not the 'thinking' part of the brain; it does not have the ability to reason or question the information that flows into it. Thinking takes place in your conscious mind, as discussed in the previous chapter, and the subconscious mind simply accepts all information from the conscious mind. As it frees up your conscious mind to deal with day-to-day life, your subconscious mind is essential for your functioning and survival.

Once information has been processed and filtered in the conscious mind, it proceeds through to the subconscious for 'storage'. While this information is being filed, the subconscious mind is unaware of the source from which it was gathered - it only knows the information is present. The subconscious mind trusts the conscious mind and relies upon it heavily. The source of information is never challenged or questioned; it is accepted as real, valid and important.

Taking the time to understand how your subconscious mind operates will greatly enhance your life, enabling you to have ample control over what you do and how you do it.

The subconscious mind has three distinct functions:

1. The operating system of the body: regulating all of the processes for human life, such as breathing and heart rate.

2. A storage vault: storing all information, images, experiences, etc. that you have ever been exposed to.

3. Regulator of the majority of your behaviour: calling on programs and beliefs that have been created through input into your conscious mind and stored in your subconscious mind.

1. Your body's operating system

As we know, the subconscious mind regulates all of your body's functions that occur 'automatically'. You do not have to use your limited attention and focus to keep your body functioning - it controls and regulates your heart functions, digestive system, body temperature and the myriad of other functions vital for your survival.

2. A storage vault of information

The subconscious mind is best described as a giant storage vault. Every bit of information that has entered your conscious mind from the moment of conception is stored in your subconscious mind. Everything you have seen, heard or experienced throughout your life is stored - nothing has been lost; it was merely stored away in your subconscious. Through hypnosis, your subconscious mind equips you with the ability to access every image, experience and sound to which you have ever been exposed.

3. Regulator of your behaviour, based on your genes, values and programs

In addition to storing all your life experiences, your subconscious mind contains all your programs (also known as beliefs) and values. Throughout this book, we will refer to these beliefs as your 'programs'. Through drawing on these programs, the subconscious mind gains the ability to control and regulate your behaviour, much the same way it controls and regulates your body's automatic functions. Furthermore, this occurs automatically without you even being consciously aware of it.

3.1 Genetics versus experience (or) nature versus nurture.

A portion of who you are and how you behave is due to your genetic predisposition. Your genes not only influence how much you look like your parents or whether you have Great Uncle Fred's nose, they also affect how you feel, behave and react to certain situations.

At the time of your birth, you were a blank canvas. Your mind was unfilled and clear from any pre-existing or outside influences; clear from any programs, beliefs or values. However, your genetic predisposition was present from the time of your conception and contributes to who you are today.

From the moment of conception, you became a sponge, drawing in information from the environment around you. As you grew and the years passed, beliefs, values, habits and programs started forming. This process of creating who you are through programming your subconscious mind and interacting with your genes will continue until the end of your time on earth.

3.2 What is a program?

The word 'Program' is defined in the dictionary as: A plan of action to accomplish a specific end; the way something is done. Your 'programs', as stated previously, refer to your habits, beliefs and values stored in your subconscious mind. In other words, they refer to everything that is stored in your subconscious mind that controls the 'way in which you do things'. These programs contribute significantly to who you are today, the way in which you behave when faced with a specific situation and how you see yourself and the world.

3.3 How were your programs created in the first place?

Throughout your life, but especially during early childhood between birth and six years of age, your subconscious mind is creating programs to assist your conscious mind in functioning. Information constantly enters your conscious mind through your senses. However, because there is a constant demand on your conscious mind which is limited in capacity, it relies heavily on your subconscious mind to alleviate the amount of information it has to remember and the number of activities it is responsible for executing. Your subconscious mind assists your conscious mind by creating 'programs' that regulate your behaviour automatically, in the same way it regulates all your bodily functions automatically. These programs are created when the same information flows into the conscious mind repeatedly. Programs are created using information such as what your parents say to you, your peers' responses to you and life experiences. The subconscious mind takes over by creating a program, freeing up your conscious mind from having to deal with the same information again and again.

For example, three-year-old Billy strives to learn basic addition. However, he experiences some difficulty remembering how to add 2 + 2. Noticing his struggle, Billy's father tells Billy he is stupid. As Billy continues attempting to remember simple addition, his father repeatedly comments on his struggle, thus making him feel worthless and dumb. Billy's subconscious mind creates a program so he no longer needs to consciously remember he is bad at maths. The program created in Billy's subconscious mind says, "I am bad at maths". Billy proceeds to grow up with a program that says he is not good at maths.

Human beings always behave in a manner consistent with their programs. Your programs direct your behaviour every minute of every day. Throughout Billy's life, he behaves in a manner consistent with his program; always performing badly at maths. Even when he attempts to do maths, he is prevented from performing well, as it would be inconsistent with his subconscious program. As an adult, Billy is confronted with a maths problem. However, his subconscious program saying, "I am bad at maths", runs automatically. Billy decides to not even attempt the maths problem in the belief he will not be able to work it out.

Conversely, if a child is told he is very studious, a subconscious program saying, "I am studious" is created. The child always behaves in a manner consistent with his program and proceeds to engage with life as someone who is diligent, eager to learn, eager to attempt problems and willing to ask questions when he doesn't understand something. This manner of behaving reinforces the program that he is studious. In this example, the child's program is working to his benefit. In Billy's example, the same principle of programming applies, but the program in Billy's mind is not setting him up for success, in fact it will impact his life negatively.

Irrespective of whether your programs are beneficial or not, they guide and direct your behaviour. You will always behave in a manner consistent with your subconscious programs.

Programs are created in your subconscious mind through repetition. When the same information repeatedly enters your conscious mind, your subconscious mind forms a program consistent with the information entering your conscious mind, thus freeing up your conscious mind's capacity for dealing with other information.

Programs can also be created instantly when associated with a strong emotional experience or state. So if you are very upset, fearful or even elated, any information entering your conscious mind while you are in this heightened emotional state could form a program instantly. For example, Johnny, at age five was told he was a 'stupid little boy' only once, while he was crying and feeling very upset. The program 'I am a stupid little boy' formed instantly in his subconscious mind and will remain there to regulate his behaviour for the rest of his life, until he reprograms his own mind for success.

When you are confronted with a specific situation, your subconscious mind automatically runs the corresponding pre-programmed response, directing and guiding your behaviour. You will then behave and respond to this situation in a pre-programmed manner. You will not be consciously aware of the fact that your behaviour is being directed by your subconscious programming and probably will not have a conscious awareness of how you behave, just as you are not currently aware of how many times your heart is beating as you read this sentence. As long as Billy lives with the program that he is not good at maths, he will always behave as if he is not good at maths. His behaviour will reinforce this program. The function of his conscious mind, perception, will filter out any evidence contrary to his program (or belief), maintaining and strengthening this bad program contained in his subconscious mind.

No matter what situation in which you find yourself, you will always behave in a manner consistent with your subconscious programs. Your subconscious programs run in the background and direct your behaviour, leaving your conscious mind free to deal with the information that is present at any point in time. Of these programs you have three kinds, the 'technical terms' for these programs are: Good programs, Okay programs and Bad programs.

YOU are not your programs

YOU are not your mind. YOU are also not your subconscious programming. YOU are a Spiritual Being having a human experience. YOU have been given a subconscious mind to assist YOU in functioning as a human being.

However, the way in which you see yourself is very heavily influenced by your subconscious programming. Self-image is the term used to describe who you think you are, what you think about yourself and how you feel about yourself and your place in the world. It is important to understand that if you do not have a good self-image at the moment, it is probably due to the fact that you have a few bad programs running in your subconscious mind.

Even though you are bound by the manner in which your mind operates, you do not need to be a prisoner of any bad programs contained in your subconscious mind. Through enlisting the same process used to create your existing programs, YOU, as a Spiritual Being, can take responsibility for programming your mind for success. You have the ability to reprogram and control your mind and ensure every program contained in your subconscious mind is good, creating a good self-image in the process. Your current programming is responsible for much of your behaviour, your successes and/or failures, as well as much of what you consider to be you. Taking control of your programming is essential in becoming the powerful and best YOU. You cannot be the powerful YOU while you have unproductive or bad programs stored in your subconscious mind. Good programming allows you to feel good about yourself and perform well effortlessly every time.

3.4 Take control of your mind, take control of your life

As an adult, it is your responsibility to take control of the programming contained in your subconscious mind, so you can have an extraordinary life and contribute to the world in a meaningful manner. In order to do this, you need to program your subconscious mind with programs for success. Much of what you currently consider to be 'you' is in actual fact not 'you'. Much of what you believe to be you, what you believe about yourself and the world, and much of how you behave is the result of your subconscious programming. Your subconscious programs are not who you are!

The secret to reprogramming your subconscious mind

Reprogramming your mind is surprisingly easy! It is a three-step process you can employ immediately to program your mind for success. Success being defined as: being the powerful, best YOU and living an extraordinary life.

Start to program and reprogram your mind for success now!

Step 1: Define the good programs that will allow you to be your best and live extraordinarily. Create a list of all of the attributes you want to have and all the programs and beliefs that will ensure success.

Step 2: Input these new programs into your conscious mind repeatedly by saying, listening to, writing and visualising these new programs.

Step 3: Incorporate this process into your daily routine and be disciplined at reprogramming your subconscious mind.

The three steps explained

To easily reprogram your subconscious mind for success, you must simulate the process involved in creating your current programs in the first place. The greatest advantage of this process is you get to choose your own programs! You are no longer reliant on your parents, peers, teachers and other people to program you. The first step is to decide which programs you need running in your subconscious mind to ensure you are the powerful YOU and that you live an extraordinary life (success). You must define your own good programs that will ensure success. Once you have programmed your subconscious mind with these programs for success, you will behave in a manner consistent with these programs without having to remember to do so. Through behaving successfully, being the powerful YOU and living extraordinarily, you will constantly reinforce your good programs. Your perception will also assist in the process by only allowing you to see the evidence that fits with your good programming. This will ensure the process your mind employs will work to your benefit!

There are simple rules you need to follow when defining the best 'you' statements that you will use in creating your good programs. You must state your defined programs in the first person, present tense and ensure they are positive. These statements, called your personal power statements, will describe who you will become through the process of programming your subconscious mind.

Beware: the last thing you want to do is inadvertently program your subconscious mind with more bad programs. Avoid statements containing the words 'not, don't and can't'. Sometimes you will need to be creative with your words to express yourself in a positive manner. An example of this would be:

Bad statement: I don't care what other people think of me.
Good personal power statement: I am free of the opinions of others!

The length of your personal power statements can vary; however short statements work very well. Selecting general attributes that will apply to different aspects of your life is also beneficial. You can be as specific or general as you please. Also, it is not uncommon for someone to have 200 personal power statements; why not program your subconscious mind with as many good pro grams as you can? Creating an extraordinary life folder (further discussed in chapter 11) that contains these personal power statements for easy reference works exceptionally well.

Your personal power statements should generally start with 'I am... '
Personal power statement examples:

> ✓ I am kind.
>
> ✓ I am loving.
>
> ✓ I am confident.

✓ I am happy.

✓ I feel good about myself.

✓ I am tremendous.

✓ I am healthy.

✓ I am a great ….(your occupation).

✓ I am an outstanding mother.

✓ I am an outstanding father.

✓ I am a leader.

✓ I am friendly.

✓ I am energetic.

✓ I am active.

✓ I take initiative.

✓ I am feeling good.

✓ I am efficient.

✓ I am decisive.

To assist you in making this process as easy as possible, please go to www.nakedtruthaboutyou.com for a list of universal power statements that will start you off in the process of reprogramming your subconscious mind for success.

The second step is to repeatedly input these personal power statements into your conscious mind through your senses until your new programs are created (this is the same manner in which your programs were created initially). Through repetition, these small personal statements will create new powerful programs in your subconscious mind, setting you up for success.

The secret is this: the process does not work if you fail to repeatedly input your personal power statements into your conscious mind. The more effort you put into entering these statements into your conscious mind through any of the processes discussed below, the faster your new programs will develop in your subconscious mind.

Generating emotion also speeds up the creation of your new programs. Remember, programs are created instantly if you are in a highly emotional state. Take advantage of this fact by generating as much emotion in your body as possible when entering these personal power statements into your conscious mind.

Enter the statements into your conscious mind in the following ways:

1. Declare or affirm your personal power statements by saying them out loud. Repeat each statement at least five times twice daily, boldly declaring who you are – the powerful you!

2. Write these statements out repeatedly. This is especially effective when done first thing in the morning. However, just write them whenever you have the opportunity.

3. Imagine (visualise) your personal power statements as true. Take time to see, feel and hear yourself, in your mind, being the powerful YOU by applying these statements to your life.

4. Create an audio CD containing your personal power statements and listen to it daily. This is a very easy and effective way to ensure continuous input of your personal power statements into your conscious mind.

5. Generate strong emotions during the above process to aid in the creation of your new programs.

6. It is really that easy! Start creating your good programs now!

What happens to your existing programs?

As stated before, you currently hold good, okay and bad programs in your subconscious mind. By following the process described above, you will strengthen your good programs and replace the okay and bad programs. However, it is unlikely you will define every possible program you need in your life. Because 94% of your behaviour and functioning is subconscious, you are not consciously aware of most of your subconscious programming. Even after years of reprogramming your subconscious mind, you might still uncover bad programs in your subconscious mind. Finding bad programs that need modifying is an ongoing process. As time passes and you grow in self-awareness, you will become better at recognising your bad programs and replacing them with good programs.

So what should you do when you uncover a bad program?

Previously, your programming came from other people and the environment, but by completing this process you are taking back the control and the responsibility for creating your programs.

Firstly, you need to recognise and identify these bad beliefs. Secondly, you need to decide what you want and determine a better program. Define your new personal power statement, ensuring it is stated in the present, first person, in a positive expression. For example, "I am a confident cook", "I am a leader", "I am a good speaker" or whatever you need to be.

By doing this, you are already starting the reprogramming sequence. Apply the same three-step process as discussed in detail previously.

As a result of your mind operating in a predictable and consistent fashion, you have the opportunity to take full advantage of its functioning. Thankfully, your subconscious mind regulates your bodily functions, acts as a storage vault for superfluous information and regulates much of your behaviour, leaving your conscious mind with the capacity to deal with your day-to-day life. You now have the ability to ensure the process it relies on is working to your benefit by creating good programs in your subconscious mind and overwriting bad programs; thus enabling you to be the powerful YOU and live an extraordinary life.

CHAPTER 6

Understand the Basics of Emotions

The second tool YOU, as
a Spiritual Being, have
been given for your
human experience is
your emotions.

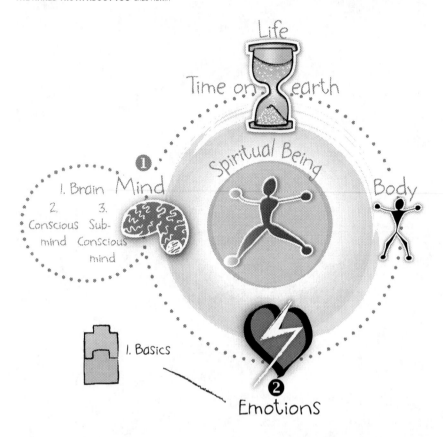

YOU are not your emotions. YOU are a spiritual being having a human experience. Your emotions are a key element to understanding yourself and your life. Mastering your emotions is an essential element for being the powerful and best YOU and living a celebrated life.

The Sixteen emotion basics YOU should know:

1. What are emotions anyway?

The word emotion refers to the way you feel every moment of every day. So, how are you feeling today? Good? Bad? You are likely to answer this question by saying you are feeling good, okay, bad or sad. Most people have very little awareness of how or what they are feeling at any given moment. The description of how you exactly feel will elude you until you pay conscious attention to it. The emotion you are feeling right now is largely subconscious, which means you are only vaguely aware of how you are feeling. The only conscious awareness you have will be whether you are feeling good (a pleasant emotion) or feeling bad (an unpleasant or uncomfortable emotion).

Emotions themselves are complicated. What one person may describe as being happy, another could identify as joyful. No matter what you feel, in all cases, emotions form the building blocks of your experience of your life and your environment.

2. What is driving the quality and experience of your life?

You 'experience' your life through your emotions. How you feel not only determines the experience of your life, but also the quality of the life you are living. You cannot have a great life whilst experiencing prevailing feelings of negativity and sadness at the same time. This will only make your life less fulfilling. Do you constantly experience unpleasant feelings of anger over your current work situation, guilt for borrowing money from the children's bank accounts and feel overwhelmed by the growing number of bills around you? These are all common feelings, but unless you take control of your emotions, they will prevent you from living a great life. Feeling anxious or fearful most of the time does not constitute being your best and living your best life.

Your emotions create your Inner-world experience, forming the basis of how you feel about yourself, your life and your environment. The emotions you feel ultimately play a major role in how you experience life and determine your quality of life. Prevailing feelings of wellbeing, happiness and peace increase the quality and experiences of your life. Alternatively, prevailing feelings of dread, depression or fear, will obviously lead to the decline of your experiences and quality of life. You cannot have an extraordinary life if you feel bad, negative or sad all, or most, of the time.

Different people respond differently to different situations. Feelings and emotions are characteristic of the individual and often independent of the environment or situation. For example, some millionaires are deeply unhappy. Considering they appear to have no obvious concerns about money, job security, etc., this may seem strange. However, what you have does not determine who you are. How you feel about your life is not necessarily based on your bank balance, environment or Outer-world.

It is the feelings you experience in your body and not the situation you are currently experiencing externally that will determine the quality of your life. This is because you experience life through your feelings. What is happening to you, where you are or what others do or say, does not determine the experiences of your life. It is the emotions you feel in response to these events that will determine the experience and quality of your life. For example, two people find themselves in the desert. One person feels excited, the other terrified. Both people are in the same desert (same circumstances), however their emotional responses are very different. The quality of these two people's lives is not influenced by being in the desert, but by how they feel about being in the desert.

When you feel good, you have a good life. When your feel bad, your life experiences will be less than you deserve.

3. You have a responsibility to feel good!

You experience your life through your emotions, so to ensure you have a good life you must feel good. The quality of your life is also determined by your emotions, therefore feeling good will considerably improve the quality of your life.

You have an obligation not only to yourself, but also to your family, friends, the people you spend time with and the world in general, to feel good! Fulfilling this duty to feel good, enables you to do good and contribute in a meaningful way. When you feel good you ultimately perform better at everything you do. You were born to glorify God and to contribute to humanity and this world through the use of your unique gifts and strengths. You really cannot fully accomplish this unless you feel good!

4. How do your emotions drive your actions?

Your emotions drive the majority of your actions, even if you think you are a logical person. The vast majority of your behaviour is the result of how you feel. You may think your actions are based on logic, but the fact is your 'logic' or thinking evokes an emotion, and the emotion results in an action. Most of your behaviour is driven by your emotions. So, what drives you to get married? What allows you to start or continue an argument? What drives you to purchase a new car? In short, your emotions!

Why aren't you aware of the fact your emotions are driving your actions? Because it is a subconscious process. Your thinking evokes an emotion that results in an action or intended action. Your mind then takes over, finding a logical substantiation for your emotionally-driven action. Becoming mindful of the connection between your feelings and actions will improve your self-awareness, ultimately resulting in greater self-control.

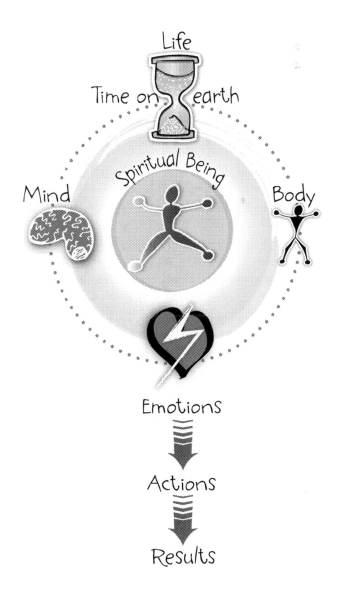

5. Good actions versus bad actions

Emotions are, in fact, only a chemical reaction within your body causing you to "feel" in a specific way. These emotions actually have no power within themselves, but they can cause you to act and react and they drive much of how you behave in any situation. Any emotion, pleasant or unpleasant, can cause you to act in one of two ways - destructively or productively.

Say you have been promoted at work. Consequently, you are feeling very happy with the outcome as you worked hard for the recognition. These feelings of happiness will cause you to behave in a specific manner. For example, you may choose to go to the pub and consume too much alcohol, causing you to get into an argument with your partner as a result of you compromising your values whilst being intoxicated. Conversely, you may choose to take your partner out for dinner, to celebrate your promotion together.

Alternatively, a setback at work can incite feelings of worry and anxiety. These feelings can cause you to become grumpy, snap at those around you and withdraw from your colleagues, family and friends. Or, you can use these same two negative feelings to fuel positive action to get yourself back on track. The emotions caused by a setback can have remarkable power. They can fuel your future progress by compelling you to analyse the current situation, set smart goals, rework your action plan, ignite activity and prevent any future disaster from occurring.

6. Your Emotional 'Danger Zone' – EDZ

Have you noticed that when your conscious mind feels overwhelmed and overloaded with demands, pressure, information and or stimuli from your environment, or when things are 'going wrong', your body automatically responds by pushing you into your Emotional Danger Zone or EDZ? An EDZ occurs when circumstances in your environment cause you to feel extremely stressed, pressured, powerless or overwhelmed.

As soon as you enter your EDZ, you will automatically act emotionally and inappropriately.

When you allow your emotions to get the better of you, you end up having an emotional outburst, saying and doing things you will regret later. Acting out whilst in your 'danger zone' is often detrimental to your relationships. Your behaviour may cause other people to feel that you are emotional and incon-sistent. Other people then begin to feel unsafe around you; feeling that your behaviour is volatile and unpredictable.

This is where self-awareness is imperative. By getting to know yourself well enough, you can recognise the early stages of when you are entering your Emotional Danger Zone. As soon as you recognise the potential causes, take steps to ensure you avoid your EDZ or manage and control your emotional re-sponses at all times.

When you are in your EDZ, the best practical way to deal with the emotions is by strenuous and vigorous exercise; it rids the body of built-up emotional en-ergy and tension. Also, to deal with the issue that triggered the stress, define your goals, create an action plan, prioritise and take the necessary action.

7. Do other people really like you?

This is an age-old question and one you have probably considered repetitively throughout your life. Such questioning can occur especially when you are feel-ing down about the world and yourself. Do others like you, and if not, what can you do to ensure you are accepted and liked?

The answer is simple: people like other people who evoke a pleasant emo-tional response in them; they like to be around people who make them feel good, safe and comfortable. If other people like the way they feel while in your company, you will become very popular. Your partner will enjoy spending time with you if he/she likes the way he/she feels about himself/herself when he/she is with you. The key element in winning people over is to make them feel good when they are in your company. Doing this will make you very popular indeed!

Remember that other people are generally very good at knowing if you are sincere when you interact with them. So, if you sincerely care about others and show true respect, interest and empathy, you will be liked.

Avoiding and controlling your EDZs and being consistent in your behaviour is essential to making other people feel good in your presence. Consistency and predictability make people feel safe.

Can others feel good when they are with you if you do not feel good about yourself? If you do not feel good about yourself, it will be difficult for others to feel good about themselves when they are around you. Therefore, ensure that other people feel good in your company by feeling good about yourself.

8. So what is real and what is imagined?

Take a moment to imagine you are sitting in your boss's office. The company you work for is currently undergoing a major restructure and your position has been cut. You are about to be informed whether you will be promoted, or made redundant…

How do you feel now? Nervous? Afraid? Excited about the possibility of a promotion? As discussed in chapter 4 (Imagination), your body cannot distinguish between reality and your imagination or thoughts. Even though this scenario is not real, it still evoked an emotional response within your body, showing that your emotions have a hard time distinguishing between real situations in your environment and imagined scenarios in your mind.

You can choose to use this process to your advantage or your disadvantage. One of the advantages is, through the productive use of your imagination, you have the ability to go anywhere and do anything in your mind, generating good feelings as a result. This process is also known as visualisation, where a person projects themself into a different situation in their mind. The same applies when you remember a funny story or situation that causes you to feel happy and joyful, resulting in laughter. By imagining your environment in many different ways, you can have the same feelings you would if your visualisation was real. What an awesome tool to assist you in having an extraordinary life!

Conversely, you can cause yourself to feel unpleasant emotions by entertaining negative thoughts, such as imagining negative scenarios for your future, or dwelling on the mistakes of the past. You can cause yourself to worry and make yourself feel terrible by dwelling on everything that is 'wrong' in your life and in the world. If you then add to this way of thinking the thoughts of powerlessness, where you have no control over your mind and environment, you will feel anxious, depressed and completely overwhelmed.

Remember, every minute of every day you have a choice to think productive thoughts and feel good, so what are you choosing to think today?

9. How does your environment or outer-world affect how you feel?

Your environment or Outer-world has a profound influence on your mind, emotions and body. Even though you can and must control your mind, it takes a concerted effort to prevent a negative environment from influencing you negatively. A negative environment has the tendency to creep into your mind and body over time and it takes a lot of energy to keep that negativity from affecting you. However, only you can allow your environment to "get to you". Only you can allow what happens in your Outer-world to enter and affect your Inner-world.

It is also important to realise that your emotional response to the things that happen in your environment is not based on the reality of your environment, but on your perception of that reality. No matter how you feel towards any situation that occurs in your environment or Outer-world, your feelings are actually based on your interpretation of the event, and not the reality of the event.

As explained in chapter 4, perception is the function of your conscious mind responsible for gathering, filtering and processing information from your environment. Your interpretation of events and situations is created by your perception. Here is a reminder of the three-step process involved:

1. Your senses gather information from your environment. The information enters your mind through your senses.

2. Your brain then determines whether the information seems familiar or not and whether it fits with your programming in your subconscious mind (what you believe about the world). If the information is not familiar or doesn't fit with your programs, it is simply filtered out and stored in your subconscious mind.

3. The remaining information is then processed and, depending on your preference, is deleted, distorted or generalised during this processing. All three methods of processing are engaged at different times, but you do have a preference and will tend to rely on one method more frequently.

In the end, the function of your conscious mind - perception - does not allow you to experience the environment as it is. You are constantly reinforcing what you already feel and believe. Therefore, you don't tend to see the environment as it is, but rather as you are. For example, if you believe you are unworthy and everyone can see how incompetent you are (Inner-world thoughts and feelings), you will only allow the evidence of what you believe from your Outer-world to enter into your conscious mind. You will continue to have the same feelings of unworthiness and incompetence during every interaction with anyone you meet in your life.

The main point to remember is, that it is not what happens in your environment or Outer-world that causes your emotional response; it is your interpretation/perception of what is happening around you that evokes the feelings you have regarding your life. Therefore, by challenging your thinking and re-programming your subconscious mind, you can ensure you feel good about yourself and your life. You are ultimately in control of how you feel.

10. Triggers

Not every emotional response you experience in the present relates to the present. Have you ever heard a familiar song from your teenage years, only to feel the same emotions you did as a teenager when you listened to the particular song? Or have you smelt a specific smell that took you back to your childhood years visiting your grandmother's kitchen? These are called triggers as they trigger a specific emotional response in your body that relates to a past experience. People, places, sounds, smells, etc. can all act as triggers.

Be aware of your triggers. Avoid triggers that evoke negative emotional experiences (if they are able to be avoided), as they do not add to the quality and experience of your life. Also take care to examine whether the emotion you might be experiencing in the present relates to a past experience; remembering that that was then, and this is now.

Note: If you find a trigger you cannot avoid, seek counselling to overcome the corresponding unpleasant emotional response.

11. Your emotions are the link between your mind and your body

Go back to the last time when you were sad. What did your body do in response? Did you complain? Did you feel tired and weak? Did you have a frown on your face, maybe tears running down your cheeks? Conversely, remember the happiest day of your life. Is that thought making you feel happy? Are you smiling (your body's corresponding reaction to happy thoughts and happy feelings)?

Your emotions are a direct link between your mind and body. When your mind has a thought, your body will respond accordingly. As a result, when you have a happy experience, your body will respond, causing you to feel happy by making you smile.

The opposite effect is also true. When you smile, even if you feel down or upset, your emotions start to respond accordingly and you will begin to feel happier. As you start to feel happier, your mind will begin producing thoughts that are more optimistic and productive. Looking up and lifting your head will help you smile even when you don't feel like smiling.

12. Why do you resist change?

Most people resist and dislike change. No matter what kind of change you intend for your life, even knowing it will be for the better, the idea of change will most likely initially evoke an unpleasant emotional response. Simply thinking about change will probably make you feel uncomfortable - even if the change will vastly improve your life or current situation.

Most people will fight to stay within their comfort zone, even when their comfort zone is a very unpleasant and uncomfortable place to exist. The term 'comfort zone' is very misleading, as most people's comfort zone is not comfortable at all. Comfort zone is the term used to describe the environment and circumstances that are familiar and predictable. Even prisoners have a comfort zone within prison. Abused spouses have a comfort zone in their home and within their abusive relationship, not because it is pleasant and comfortable, but because it is familiar and predictable.

You have a comfort zone that you try to protect from changing. Please examine your comfort zone, and if it is not a place where the powerful YOU can flourish and live well, you must change it. In most instances, you will generally try to avoid changing your comfort zone, not because of fear of change, but because you want to avoid the initial unpleasant emotions and feelings that change always evokes. Rest assured, the unpleasant emotions associated with change will soon disappear as you work to create a comfort zone that celebrates you. Unpleasant emotions will soon make way for a new and pleasant comfort zone where you can be the best powerful YOU and live well.

13. You have a thinking-feeling addiction dominating your Inner-world

Through repetitively thinking the same thoughts, your mind establishes highly strengthened connections in your brain. These connections are so well worn they become like an accustomed footpath on which you continue to walk over and over again. These footpaths become ingrained thought patterns or prominent thoughts in your mind, evoking the same emotional response every time you are faced with the same thoughts. This thinking-feeling addiction becomes your mental 'comfort zone'.

Problems occur when the thinking-feeling addiction (your prominent thoughts) becomes negative, leaving you feeling depressed and anxious. Unfortunately, many people experience this negative thinking-feeling addiction and, as this pattern becomes familiar, it becomes their comfort zone. This comfort zone is reinforced every time the pattern and prominent thought is repeated. Any change to this thinking-feeling pattern takes a concerted effort on your part, because as stated earlier, your natural response is to resist change. However, it is in your best interest to make this change.

Changing will be much easier if you generate dissatisfaction with your present situation and create a vision or belief for an improved future. Incorporating these two elements into your thinking will assist you in choosing to change.

So how do you change this thinking-feeling pattern if it constantly leaves you feeling down? There are a number of things you can do and each of them takes an initial concerted and conscious effort on your part, but when you succeed, your extraordinary life is on its way! The best way to evoke change is to:

- Become aware of your thoughts.
- Interrupt any negative thought immediately and replace it with a counter thought – a positive personal power statement.
- Repeat or recite this positive personal power statement constantly, resisting the return of the negative thought by focussing on your positive personal power statement.

- Create a new positive thinking-feeling addiction by developing positive thought connections in your mind. This is done in the same way as negative thought patterns were first established – through repetition.

- Repeatedly use the strength of your will to resist negative thoughts and replace them immediately with positive personal power statements.

Remember, a personal power statement is saying and thinking good things about yourself to yourself. By repeating only good and positive things about yourself, you will begin to notice a different emotional response within, allowing you to view your life from a more positive perspective and more productive prominent thoughts.

14. Another reason to embrace change

One of the reasons you were given life here on earth is to grow from immaturity to maturity. However, you cannot both grow and stay the same as you are now - growth always involves change. Therefore, your life will be so much better if you decide to embrace change and learn to become familiar with the feelings associated with change.

Any unpleasant 'change emotions' you feel are your friends, because they are an indication that you are doing something different with your life - that you are changing. By learning to recognise these emotions, you will discover a way to welcome and befriend them. Feel and embrace the unpleasant 'change' emotions as the evidence that you are changing, growing and becoming the powerful YOU!

15. Why do you procrastinate?

Procrastination is not avoiding a particular activity or situation, it is avoiding the unpleasant feelings you associate with the activity or situation. The secret to overcoming procrastination is more often than not to deal with the situation or activity regardless of the uncomfortable emotions you might experience. Apply your will. You can feel the emotion and do it anyway…

16. You can feel it and do it anyway...

Regardless of what you feel at any given time, you have the power to continue to do it nevertheless. Therefore, when you feel fearful about doing a new activity, instead of running away, you can choose to go ahead and do it. The only thing stopping you is you!

Consider dancers waiting backstage to perform. For weeks they have rehearsed and practiced, all the while experiencing ever-growing emotions of anxiety and nervousness. Nevertheless, on the opening night, they enter the stage ready to perform. Even though fearful of performing, the fear they felt was 'good fear' - it gave them the courage to push through the fear and dance their very best.

Even when you feel sad, you have the power to smile. Only you have the choice to turn your emotions around. While the sadness you feel may be all consuming, you cannot allow it to control your life. By smiling, you are not allowing your sadness to take over; you are taking back control.

One of the most important steps you will have to take in becoming the powerful YOU is feeling the fear and doubt but taking the action anyway. Believe in your dreams, your plans, yourself, your life and your future – moving boldly in the direction of the best YOU and your best life will always take courage. Without fear there is no courage.

Mastering your emotions

This insight gained into your emotions will make you more powerful. Knowing yourself and being mindful of all the different elements of your emotions gives you the ability to master and control this powerful tool. When you master and control your emotions, you master and control your actions and inadvertently master and control the results you will achieve in your life.

CHAPTER 7

Feel Good!

Activity = Results
Emotions drive Activity

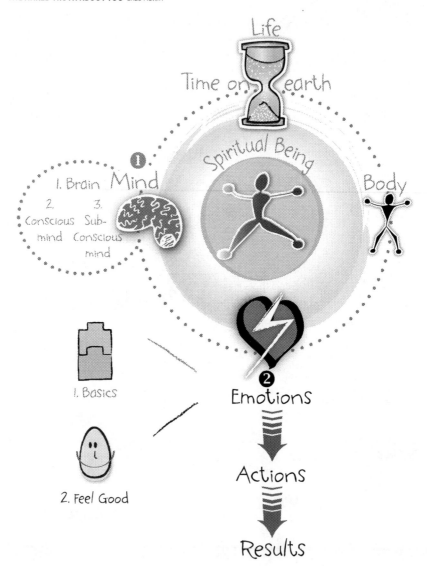

The life you are living today is the summation of all the actions you have or have not taken over time. Many experts are now saying the results you achieve in your life are the direct result of the total sum of all the thinking you have done; where everything you have ever thought has guided you to where you are today. In a way this is true, but what is more true is the fact that those thoughts evoked feelings or emotions. These emotions were the drivers of your actions and your actions produced your current results.

For example, if you had acted on any number of the good ideas you had conjured up in the past, your life would be significantly different today. Some of those good ideas were probably accompanied by thoughts of doubt that caused you to feel fearful and insecure and it was these emotions that prevented you from acting on your thoughts. Therefore, if action produces results, and your action is fuelled by your emotions, it is crucial to ensure you have control over your emotions.

Thinking ⟫➡ Feeling ⟫➡ Activity ⟫➡ Result

You have a responsibility to feel good!

When you feel good, you are ultimately better at everything you do. Good feelings drive good actions. You become a better person, husband, wife, friend, family member, colleague, citizen etc. As a result of feeling good, your relationships improve, you are better at your job and you are more willing and able to contribute to the world. When your emotions are scattered everywhere and you feel overwhelmed and stressed, it prevents you from being and doing your best. The best YOU is not the stressed you.

The world is crying out for more joyful, positive people who are doing good things with their lives. It is your responsibility to ensure you are living your life to the fullest by making sure the prevailing emotions you are feeling are positive and productive ones. Without feeling good most of the time, you are not able to make your unique and best contribution to the world and its people.

Lasting or prevailing unpleasant emotions drain you of your most valuable resources – your energy, attention, power, strength and focus. Let's face it, the world does not need another negative, pessimistic, unhappy or overwhelmed person; there are too many like that in the world as it is. Your life, family, colleagues, friends and your world all need you to feel good!

But isn't it selfish or indulgent to feel good all of the time?

The answer is NO! It is time now for you to feel GOOD! What a freeing truth! Feeling good is not indulgent, nor selfish; it is your responsibility. When you feel good, you can ultimately contribute and help other people more. That is not selfish; it is imperative.

Your prevailing emotions should be feelings of wellbeing, happiness and gratitude. You should be feeling good in the knowledge your life has meaning. You have embarked on the journey of mastering your Inner-world, your mind, emotions and body, enabling you to have control over your life.

But shouldn't other people work harder to make you feel good?

It is ultimately your responsibility to feel good. Do not wait for your circumstances to change, do not wait until you get married, do not wait for the promotion, do not wait for everybody else to change so you can stay the same. Decide to do whatever it takes to feel good now! If you can start to work towards feeling good right now, things can only get better from here on!

It is only you who can insist on feeling good. You are ultimately responsible for and able to do what it takes to make yourself feel good. You are entirely capable of controlling yourself and your life. You might have relinquished control by giving your power away to others, but the time has come to regain control over yourself - regain your power and start feeling good!

Why should you insist on feeling good?

When you feel good within yourself, the way you view your environment, your life and the world is significantly different from when you feel negative. When feeling confident and happy, you are much more likely to also feel energetic and take action to get the most out of your life. In contrast, when feeling depressed and overwhelmed, the most you feel like doing is staying in bed doing nothing all day. When you feel insecure or threatened, you will probably argue with your family and friends or avoid them altogether.

It is vital to feel good about yourself and your life, for when you do, your performance improves in all aspects. When you feel good, you do good because you experience your life through your emotions. Don't you want a good life? A good life is a life of feeling good. Feeling good on the inside guarantees your experience of life is good, irrespective of your circumstances. This is great news, because only you have the control to insist on feeling good. Only you have the power to ensure you feel good over time and only you can determine the thoughts and take the actions required to make yourself feel good.

How often should you feel good?

Is it realistic to say you should feel good all of the time? Isn't life filled with ups and downs? The reality is, you have an emotional state you are in most of the time. It is your emotional comfort zone – feelings you are so familiar with that they are your 'normal' feelings; the feelings you live with day to day, when your life is going through its paces.

You should feel good 90% of your life. You should learn to feel good through life's ups and downs. In fact, you should feel good daily. Your emotional comfort zone should be feeling good.

What is your 'feel-good goal'?

If I asked you to rate how good you feel at this moment on a scale of 1 – 10 (10 being feeling fantastic), what would your answer be? A 6? Maybe a 7? It might even be a 1, 2 or a 3?

The aim is to FEEL GOOD - at least 8/10. You must decide to feel good (8/10) almost every minute of every day, consistently over time.

What does it mean to feel good?

The following is a list of emotions you should be feeling the majority of the time:

✓ Gratitude

✓ Kindness

✓ Excitement

✓ Enthusiasm

✓ Passion

✓ Love

✓ Peaceful/calm

✓ Optimism

✓ Joy

✓ Hope

✓ Relief

✓ Happy

✓ Faith

✓ Control, not over others but over yourself – Self control

✓ Confident

✓ Well

✓ Contentment

✓ Strong

✓ Well-being

✓ Safe

✓ Secure

✓ Feeling that all will turn out well

✓ Enthusiasm

✓ Drive

✓ Control

✓ Courage

✓ Focus

✓ Energetic

✓ Personal power

✓ Compassion

24 Practical strategies for feeling GOOD!

If you have a responsibility to feel good, then what can you do to guarantee you feel good 90% of the time? Below are 24 practical feel-good strategies. These strategies are simple and easy to follow. However, they will only work if you implement them into your daily routine, so take control of your emotions by incorporating these strategies into your daily schedule.

1. Decide

Feeling good starts with a decision. It is a decision you might have to make repeatedly, maybe hourly at first. You must decide that you WILL FEEL GOOD, regardless of what is going on in your life. You must decide that it is important to feel good and that you will not tolerate anything less than feeling good. You have one life and the choice between feeling good or feeling negative. Why would you choose to feel negative if you could feel good instead? Choose to take responsibility for how you feel! Choose to feel good regardless of where you are, who you are with and what your circumstances are. You can always choose to feel good in any situation. Be strong willed about feeling good!

Viktor Frankl was a Jewish psychiatrist who lived through the Second World War. He endured years of tremendous hardship and horror in the Nazi death camps. During this time, he developed an incredible insight into humanity. One of his remarkable revelations was that, as a human being, you always have a choice. There are times when you are not able to choose your circumstances, but you can ALWAYS choose how you feel in and about those circumstances.

Every situation you are in offers a choice – you can always choose your thoughts, your attitudes and your feelings. Just like Viktor Frankl chose to find meaning in the midst of unspeakable horror, you also can choose to find meaning in your life, ensuring you feel good.

2. Be grateful

You can choose to feel good immediately by thinking about what is good in your life. Focusing on what you have creates feelings of gratitude. Feeling grateful results in feeling good. Every person living in the developed world has many reasons to feel grateful. You have so much!

Stop comparing yourself to the Jones's. Compare yourself to the majority of people alive today. Let's really put your life into perspective:

According to the World Bank (www.worldbank.org)
- 8 million people die annually because they are simply too poor to stay alive.

- More than 800 million people go hungry daily.

- Approximately 9.2 million children under the age of five die annually; mostly from preventable diseases.

- 2.8 billion people live in poverty daily. They exist on less than $2 a day.

- Chances are, you have a lot to be grateful for!

Create a Gratitude Journal where you write at least seven things for which you are grateful each day – it can be something as simple as bread or your breakfast cereal, or as profound as life itself. Focus on each one and generate feelings of gratitude. The first step towards achieving more is being grateful for what you already have.

3. Laugh
Laughter is the best medicine. Numerous medical studies have been conducted about the effects of laughter. Research indicates that when you laugh, you boost your immune system, lower your blood pressure, reduce the stress hormones in your body and, most importantly, release endorphins. These endorphins are your body's natural painkillers and 'feel good' hormones that will give you a natural sense of well being.

Make laughter a priority in your life and laugh heartily every day. Create laughing opportunities and set yourself a goal of daily laughing out loud with your family.

4. Exercise
Daily rigorous exercise for just 10-15 minutes will rid your body of built up tension as well as release more endorphins. Exercise will not only enable you to maintain your general feel-good attitude and reduce stress, anxiety and built-up tension, it will also ensure your body is strong and healthy.

Everybody is busy, but nobody is too busy to incorporate 15 minutes of exercise into their daily routine. The goal is to exercise 15 minutes a day, 6 days a week, every week of the year for the rest of your life. Set yourself up to succeed by making your exercise goals sustainable and achievable. Be honest, you have 15 minutes a day spare; make the best use of your time by exercising.

5. Breathe

Negative emotions often affect your breathing, causing it to become shallow and fast. Not breathing effectively will then add to the discomfort you will experience in these situations. Remember to breathe effectively, especially when under pressure or in a stressful situation.

Implement a simple breathing technique:

Begin breathing in and out slowly, concentrating on how the air enters and leaves your lungs; then allow your body to relax with each increasing breath. After about seven to ten deep breaths, change your focus from the negativity surrounding you to the positive. Mentally picture the negative thoughts leaving your body every time you exhale, replacing each one with a personal power statement as you inhale. Repeat this as often as needed.

6. Sleep

Five interesting facts about sleeping and *not* sleeping are:

- Sleeping disorders cost the developed world's economy billions of dollars each year. The cost of sleeping disorders to the Australian economy in 2004 was $10.3 billion.

- Seventeen hours of wakefulness results in a significant decrease in performance, equivalent to a blood alcohol-level of 0.05%.

- Chronic insomnia impacts many aspects of a person's life including increased use of medical services, family problems, increased use of alcohol, reduced work performance and emotional problems.

- Research conducted at University College London and Warwick University discovered that a constant lack of sleep almost doubles your risk of developing heart disease.

- Sleep is vital to your functioning. Your physical and emotional wellness depends on sleeping. No matter what age you are, limited sleep can affect every aspect of your lifestyle – from work to home to personal relationships. When your body works well, you sleep well.

Nightly restful sleep ensures you feel good during the day. You cannot feel good if you are always tired or rundown. Too many people get too little sleep, resulting in them feeling dull and grumpy. Determining how much sleep is 'enough' depends on you. Work out how many hours of sleep constitute a good night's rest for you and prioritise sleeping well. If you are suffering from a sleeping disorder or disturbance, consult your doctor immediately.

7. Ensure good nutrition

Your vehicle parked outside your house or in your garage consumes fuel when it is driven. Do you take care when refuelling your vehicle? Do you fill your car with petrol if is it is a diesel car, or with diesel if it runs on petrol? You know that in order to get performance from your vehicle, you need to fill it with the appropriate fuel.

Food is your body's fuel. Consider what you are fuelling your body with by considering your diet. Is food with high sugar and salt content really the most appropriate fuel for your body? The fuel (food) you consume daily directly impacts your health, well-being and performance. What you eat contributes significantly to the way you feel about yourself.

By being mindful of what you eat and ensuring your blood sugar levels remain stable, you can be assured your mood will become more stable and positive as a result. However, if you find you are lethargic or your mood starts to shift when eating certain foods, try to avoid those foods as much as possible. It would be helpful also to consult your doctor, as you may have an undiagnosed food intolerance.

8. Take dietary supplements

Taking supplements such as fish oil and evening primrose is also an effective way to help stabilise your emotions. However, before taking any over-the-counter medication and adding them as supplements to your diet, it is advisable to speak to your doctor, pharmacist or dietician.

9. Drink water

Adequate water intake is essential. To determine how much water you need, calculate your daily water intake by multiplying 0.045 litres x your weight in kg (if you are over 50kg). The answer to this equation is what your daily fluid intake should be.

10. Control your mind

When you decide to feel good, you also inadvertently decide to reject things which negatively affect your emotions. As most thoughts result in an emotional response, you must control your mind to think only that which makes you feel good. Negative thoughts are thoughts that result in negative feelings. Reject and resist negative thoughts generated by your conscious and or subconscious mind. Replace every negative thought with a positive power statement, repeating this statement until the negative thought absconds.

Initially you will need to be disciplined in entertaining only thoughts that make you feel good, but it is well worth the effort. As you continue to resist negative thoughts and think positive thoughts, the negative thought connections in your mind will weaken and disappear over time, leaving in their place your new, positive perspective on life.

11. Run good programs

Creating and maintaining good programs in your subconscious mind is essential for your long-term happiness and success. Reprogram your subconscious mind for success by repeating positive personal power statements about yourself and your life. Refer to chapter 5 for a detailed explanation of this process. Your behaviour, thoughts and feelings will always be consistent with your subconscious programming. Good programs will make you feel good.

12. Guard what you give your attention to

Your attention and focus are two of your most limited and valuable resources. Take great care in what you give your attention to. It is hard to feel good about life when you are constantly watching criminal stories, reading horror books and downloading harmful content and images from the Internet. Be disciplined in keeping your attention on that which makes you feel good. The world is filled with both good and bad, happy and sad. By choosing to focus on that which is good, you give yourself an opportunity to feel good.

13. Learn and grow

Curiosity, the ability to explore, learn and grow brings pleasure to life. Look around you; your life and environment offers many opportunities for you to do just that.

For example, you can buy books that took hundreds of hours to write and produce, that contain thousands of thoughts, ideas and countless experiences; all for $10 - $30! Now that is a bargain.

Or you could visit your local library, free of charge. There you can travel the world through reading. You have the opportunity to learn and explore any subject of interest. Books hold so many different worlds and through reading you can learn so much, grow so much and experience so many things.

The Internet is another tremendous resource for learning. Enrolling in a course will make you part of a community of like-minded people who are also interested in bettering themselves and their life. Living in the developed world offers so many opportunities for learning and growing.

Additionally, you can learn so much by simply exploring a new park, visiting a museum, taking up a new hobby or planting a garden. The world is bursting with exciting ways in which you can learn and grow!

Commit to being a lifelong learner. Generate curiosity about something interesting daily. Expand your life through exploring, learning and growing daily.

14. Avoid negative triggers

As discussed in chapter 6, triggers are people, places, sounds, smells, etc. which evoke an emotional experience in the present that relates to a past experience. A negative trigger is anything that evokes a negative emotion in the present that relates to a negative past experience. Avoid negative triggers. For example, if listening to a specific song brings back feelings of sadness or heartbreak, avoid playing that song. The same principle applies to people, places and all other negative triggers – avoid them.

(If you are faced with an unavoidable trigger that repeatedly evokes an unpleasant emotional response, seek professional help and counselling.)

15. Music

Music evokes an emotional response. Music often plays an important part in many of the significant events in your life, like birthday parties, weddings, funerals, special dates etc. Incorporating music into more of your life is an easy way to increase your feeling of well being. Remember that the mood of a piece of music will evoke similar emotions in you. So take care to choose music with 'healthy' lyrics and subject matter and uplifting, relaxing and inspiring tunes. By playing your favourite music often and regularly, you will create a life filled with music and laughter.

16. Lend a helping hand

Helping someone is guaranteed to leave you feeling good. There are so many opportunities in your environment to offer help to someone. All you have to do is have a willing heart. Help others by doing what you love. If your enjoy baking, bake a cake for someone less fortunate than yourself. If you enjoy shopping, offer to help with an elderly person's grocery shopping. Donate, volunteer, write letters of appreciation, visit the lonely and the sick; the opportunities are endless. Regardless of what you choose to do for others, you will gain the greatest benefit.

17. Smash your shackles

Experiencing disappointment, failure and hurt is an unavoidable part of your human experience. However, while you carry and harbour hurt, disappointment and bitterness in your heart and mind, these feelings become shackles, holding you back and tying you down.

Failure is only a failure if you fail to learn from the experience. View your past failures as invaluable life lessons, empowering and preparing you for the rest of your life.

Experiencing hurt and disappointment is also a part of being human. However, holding on to these hurts and disappointment is optional. By acknowledging, letting go of and learning from past experience, you can smash the shackles that are tying you down and preventing you from fully living. This process is explained in detail in chapters 8 and 9.

18. Overcome your problems

Another integral part of your human existence is experiencing problems. Everybody faces problems at some point in their lives. If you are facing a problem now, you must engage with it vigorously and solve it as soon as possible. How to be a creative problem solver is discussed in detail in chapter 14.

You determine your own willingness and ability to overcome your problems. Engaging in your problems now and moving beyond your current situation is essential for feeling good. Overcome your challenges before they overcome you.

19. Meditate and pray

Schedule time and create a space where you can meditate and pray. Calm your mind, focus your positive intention, express gratitude for what you have and ask for what you need. This practice brings connection and inner peace. Being quiet allows you to receive answers to your questions and requests, and cultivates a positive expectation that all will turn out well, leaving you feeling optimistic and calm.

20. Set goals

Do you feel like a little boat on the ocean, being tossed to and fro with no clear direction or purpose; simply coping with what the ocean sends your way? If this describes how you feel about your life, it is an indication that you must work out what you want. You must set goals.

By setting goals, you develop a plan for your future. This plan in turn keeps you focussed on the bigger picture. When you focus on what you want, your mind will show you the opportunities available in your environment to achieve what you want. Goals define the road and enable you to move boldly in the direction of your best life.

Approximately 80% of people in the world struggle with goal setting. When confronted with the question, 'what do you want?' they are unable to answer.

How to set goals is discussed in detail in chapter 14. This will assist to set your first goals - to take charge of the direction of your life.

21. Change your words

Your words have enormous power. As you speak, you constantly predict your own future. Feeling good, being the powerful YOU and living well all depends heavily on what you say from day to day. So here is your warning: watch your words!

Changing your words will change your life. Ensure you only speak positively about yourself and your future. Be mindful of the words you choose to use. Always guard what you say and only ever state what you want in life. NEVER speak of what you don't want, as this is precisely what you will get.

The English language offers many traps for uttering what you don't want. Common phrases used daily speak about what not to do instead of what to do, for example:

Incorrect language	Correct language
Don't be late	Be on time
Don't forget	Remember…
Don't cry	Calm down / breathe
Don't fall	Stay on your feet
Don't get sick	Be healthy

Because you are constantly programming your mind and influencing the outcomes of your life by what you say on a daily basis, it is vital to ensure you are speaking positively. Do you keep saying how difficult your life is? Do you keep repeating how tired, stressed, drained and overwhelmed you are?

By doing so, you reinforce these things in your mind and your life; unwittingly programming your mind to experience every aspect of your life as being difficult, tiring, stressful and overwhelming.

Being mindful of and disciplined in only speaking of what you want will not only change how you feel, but will also change your life.

22. Encourage yourself

Have you ever asked yourself a question expecting an answer? You are not going crazy. You have a little voice talking constantly in your mind. This is just you talking to yourself, known as self-talk.

Are you continuously speaking negatively and harshly to yourself? Start by paying attention to your self-talk and uncover what it is you are repeating to yourself. Are you constantly saying how difficult, impossible and hard your job, relationships and life is? Are you in fact your harshest critic, constantly finding fault with yourself and your life? Are you trying to criticise yourself into being a better person? If your answer is yes to any of these questions, you are preventing yourself from being the best YOU and from feeling good by constantly speaking negativity into your mind.

Take control of your self-talk. Speak love, encouragement, affirmation and power into your mind and your life.

23. Find meaning in your daily activities

Your life consists of the activities and emotions of your daily routine. This routine is dotted with various significant occasions and events, like special birthdays, sad events, parties, setbacks, promotions, health concerns and wonderful celebrations. However, your daily 'mundane' routine constitutes the majority of your life.

Just because it is repetitive, your daily routine does not have to be meaningless or mundane. Every activity in your daily routine offers the opportunity to find meaning in your life. Doing something well, making someone's day, going the extra mile, and bringing love, care and a smile to everything you do creates meaning in the ordinary.

Your extraordinary life is finding meaning in your 'ordinary daily routine'. As soon as you become mindful of your life, paying attention to all that you do, you will see, feel and hear meaning in everything.

24. Love

Love ultimately gives meaning to life. Love is enduring and all encompassing. Love is the ultimate feel-good emotion. Love grows and multiplies as it is given away. Loving yourself is essential. When you truly love yourself, you have love to give. As you give love, you will receive more love in return; multiplying the love in the world. Creating loving relationships with other people will give your life meaning, enrich your life, make you feel good and make the world a better place. Love more daily!

CHAPTER 8

Gain Advantage from Unpleasant Emotional Experiences

Unpleasant emotions are not designed to spoil your life; they are designed to assist you, keep you safe, help you build relationships and facilitate personal growth and strength.

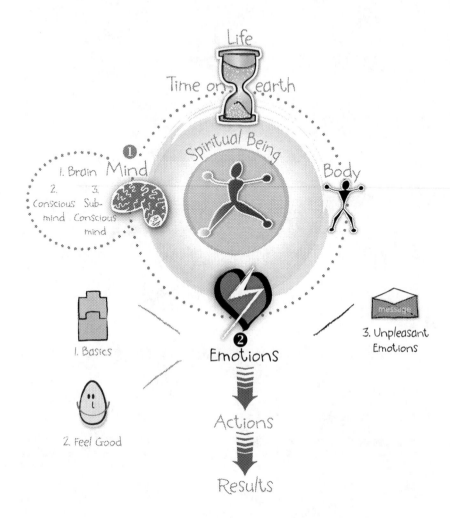

If every aspect of life is more enjoyable when you feel good, why do you have the ability to experience unpleasant emotions? Wouldn't your life be less complicated and more pleasurable if you only experienced pleasant emotions?

Unpleasant emotions are, in fact, very useful. You experience unpleasant emotions for a reason. Unpleasant emotions are not designed to spoil your life; they are designed to assist you, keep you safe, help you build relationships and facilitate personal growth and strength. However, it is essential you understand how to interpret and use these unpleasant emotional experiences to your advantage.

Why do you experience unpleasant emotions?

Occasional unpleasant emotional experiences are essential elements of a healthy life. Every unpleasant emotional experience is trying to coach you by delivering an important message to you. These experiences are designed to be unpleasant to attract your attention. You need these emotional experiences to deliver a message, either about you, your environment or your life.

The messages your unpleasant emotional experiences carry are designed to help you to:

✓ Stay safe.
✓ Build relationships with others.
✓ Become more effective and productive.
✓ Uncover bad programs in your subconscious mind.
✓ Develop personal strength and power.
✓ Grow to be the powerful YOU.

However, many people are living a less than ideal life because they are unable to interpret and implement the message their unpleasant emotions are trying to convey. This lack of knowledge is preventing them from adjusting their behaviour accordingly. Even though unpleasant emotions are meant to be fleeting experiences, many people are 'stuck' in these unpleasant states due to their inability to understand the message and/or their consequent inability to act appropriately upon the message.

Unpleasant emotions exist to help you and guide you! Any time you experience an unpleasant emotion, you should ask yourself the question, 'What is the message this unpleasant emotional experience is trying to convey?'

Understanding the message is the first step. The second essential step is to ACT upon the message. It is the action you take based on the message that will allow you to move beyond the unpleasant emotional experience into feeling good again.

What's the message?

Every unpleasant emotional experience is trying to get your attention in order to 'tell' you something. The messages your emotions carry have two purposes.

1. To indicate there may be a bad program running in your subconscious mind that needs to be replaced with a good program.

2. To carry a special message about you, your life or your environment.

This process is best understood via the following examples:

Let's assume you hear a large dog barking a few blocks away and it evokes feelings of fear. Fear is an unpleasant emotional experience that is trying to grab your attention to tell you something about yourself or your life. So after paying attention to the fear, the question you ask is, 'What is the message this feeling of fear is trying to convey?' In this case, the dog is not close by and you are in no real danger. Does your fear response indicate you have a bad program in your subconscious mind, or does your fear response carry a valid message about you, your life or your environment?

As the dog is not threatening you, your fear response in this example indicates the existence of a bad program running in your subconscious mind regarding dogs. Apparently at some time in the past, you had a bad encounter with a dog which resulted in your subconscious mind storing a program that is available within a moment's notice. When this program starts running, you suddenly become aware of the fact that 'dogs are extremely dangerous'. The message this feeling of fear is giving you is that you must replace your current bad program with a more productive one regarding dogs. Now you understand the message, it is critical you take the appropriate action based on the message. The appropriate action is: reprogram your subconscious mind. Following the process discussed in chapter 4, you should reprogram your subconscious mind with something like: 'most dogs are harmless and loving companions'.

Conversely, if you are standing face to face with a vicious dog, which is barking and showing its teeth, your emotional response will also be fear. This time, the fear emotion carries an important message about your life and environment, as the threat is real and the purpose of the message is to keep you safe. The message of fear is always, "get ready" or "prepare", and is absolutely relevant for this situation. You would prepare yourself for action; to run, call out for help or protect yourself should the dog decide to attack. Acting on these messages is critical for your safety and, therefore, reverting back to feeling good. As a result, you act appropriately by getting away from the dog or calling out for help. The unpleasant experience of fear in this instance enabled you to stay safe.

In these examples the same unpleasant emotion (fear) carried two very different and important messages. In the first scenario, the emotion of fear was not justified since there was no real threat within reach. This clearly demonstrated that the physical feelings of fear indicated a bad subconscious program.

In the second scenario, the message to get ready and prepare was real and valid, as the associated physical experience of fear was justified by a true threat.

In both scenarios, it is clear that listening to and getting a handle on the message is not sufficient; it is critical you take the appropriate action based on the message. If you understand the message and do nothing, you will remain stuck in the unpleasant emotional state. Taking the appropriate action that fits with the message will enable you to revert back to feeling good.

What do you do when you experience an unpleasant emotion?

The process of what to do when confronted with an unpleasant emotion is simple:

1. Awareness: Become aware of your unpleasant emotion and pay attention to it.

2. Identify: What is the unpleasant emotion – name it.

3. Ask: What is the message?

4. Decide: Is it pointing to a bad program or is it a message about my life?

5. Act: Take appropriate action immediately based upon the message.

6. Return to feeling good.

Firstly, become aware of experiencing an unpleasant emotion. Secondly, think about what you are feeling in order to identify and name the unpleasant emotion. Then get a handle on the message this emotion carries. You will find that the emotion is saying one of two things. The emotion is either showing you there is a bad program running in your subconscious mind and holding you back from being your best, or it is telling you something about yourself, your life or your environment. In some cases, your unpleasant emotional experience will hold both these messages simultaneously. Once you have uncovered and listened to the message, it is time to act. All unpleasant emotional experiences are telling you to do something. Taking the appropriate action based on the message will allow you to return to feeling good.

What are your unpleasant emotions telling you about your life?

As previously explained, every unpleasant emotion is either pointing to a bad program running in your subconscious mind or carrying a valid message about yourself, your life and your environment.

Bad program:

When you uncover a bad program, you must replace it with a more productive and good program by following the process outlined in chapter 5.

Valid messages about you and your life:

Below is an outline of the messages attached to most of your universal unpleasant emotional experiences. Dealing with unpleasant emotions is often challenging, especially initially as you acquire the skills to interpret and act on them. The information below is designed to simplify the process and make it as easy as possible for you.

Remember, you are not meant to be 'stuck' in an unpleasant emotional experience for long. These experiences exist to help and guide you; not to taint the experience of your life. However, it is up to you to follow the process of getting the message and taking action. You determine how long you will have to endure your unpleasant emotional experience. The sooner you take the appropriate action, the faster you will return to feeling good.

Many of the common unpleasant emotions carry particular universal messages. Fear, sadness, rejection, hurt, incompetence and loneliness are common unpleasant emotions. Below is the key to identifying and understanding the messages they convey, as well as working out the appropriate course of action to take. Please refer to this section often to assist you to understand the messages your unpleasant emotions are conveying and identify the remedial actions to take.

a. Fear

Fear is caused by the anticipation and awareness of danger coming into your life. A modern day life has not helped alleviate fear; in fact it has increased the fear within us, as we are constantly informed of the dangers lurking around us. It is often the anticipation or perception that something is dangerous or that "bad" things might happen to us, which evokes this fear.

What to do when you feel fearful:

✓ Become aware of the uncomfortable feeling or emotion in your body.

✓ Use your conscious mind to examine this emotion and identify that you are actually experiencing fear.

✓ Allow your conscious mind to discover and examine what you are fearful of.

✓ Identify if it is a rational fear linked to a real threat or a bad program running within your subconscious mind.

✓ Examine the threat by asking: 'What is the worst that could happen?'

The message:

✓ *Get ready and prepare*

If it is a Real Threat:

✓ If the threat is real, the message is: Get ready and prepare! Do everything possible to prepare for or avoid the threat.

✓ Once you have done everything possible to prepare; you need to foster an optimistic belief that all will turn out well.

If it is a Bad Program:

✓ Identify the bad program that is running in your subconscious mind.

✓ Define a more productive or successful program with which to replace it.

✓ Create a positive personal power statement, for example, 'I am safe'.

✓ Retrain your subconscious mind by repeating this positive personal power statement as often as possible, daily for a period of time, visualising yourself with the new program in your life.

✓ When an old thought presents itself, interrupt it and immediately replace it with the new positive power statement.

Fear is often the foundation for stress and scepticism. Most people find themselves fearful of criticism, failure, rejection and loss of stability. However, if you use your fear response appropriately by either retraining your subconscious mind or getting ready and taking the appropriate action to prepare, you will have nothing to fear.

For example, whenever you experience fear (and it does not point to a bad subconscious program), the message is always *get ready and prepare!* How you apply this message and identify the appropriate action to take will depend on your specific situation. For instance, when you have to sit a test and you are feeling fearful, the message of *get ready and prepare* means that you need to *prepare* for the test by studying. When you feel fearful about an upcoming performance appraisal at work, you must *get ready and prepare* for the meeting by thinking about your role, what you do well and what you need to improve on; and what you need help with and training in to improve your performance at work. This preparation will enable your performance review to be a more productive and valuable experience, bringing you back to feeling good.

It is important to remember that you can feel the fear, yet act anyway; have the courage to break through the fear that is holding you back by taking the appropriate action. Courage overcomes fear. Courage will allow you to feel good again.

b. Upset, hurt and rejection:

These unpleasant emotional experiences relate to your expectations and need for other people. They relate to how you feel other people should behave towards you or something you care about. Remember, you cannot control other people, you can only influence them. However, you can and should control yourself.

The message:

✓ *Examine your expectations and needs*

What you can do:

✓ Remember, you are always teaching people how to treat you.

✓ Examine your expectations of other people.

✓ Accept people for who they are in the present.

✓ Examine if you should allow yourself to be involved with a particular person.

✓ Treat others as you would like to be treated.

✓ Treat yourself as you want others to treat you. The way you treat yourself and feel about yourself sets the tone for how others will feel about you and how others will treat you. For example, if you want to be respected, you must first respect yourself.

c. Loneliness:

Many people suffer from loneliness. If you are lonely, not taking the appropriate action is preventing you from feeling good and contributing to the world. Take initiative, take action and feel good again.

If you feel lonely, the message is:

✓ *Build a relationship with someone!*

Here are a few suggested actions to take:

✓ Identify someone or a group with whom you can build a relationship.

✓ Start spending time with another human being.

✓ Always have something to contribute to another human being; it could be a smile, a hug or even a sympathetic ear.

✓ It is time to serve others with your gifts. For example, if you are a good cook, bake a cake to take to a local nursing home for the residents.

✓ Examine what you have to give – love, care, time – and what kind of connection you desire.

✓ Volunteer your gifts to people who would benefit from your contribution.

d. Incompetency, inadequacy and uselessness:

Feeling incompetent or inadequate is really quite exciting, as it indicates you must grow and improve your character and abilities.

The message:

> ✓ *Improve, grow and become the best, powerful YOU*

The action required:

✓ Do something that will improve your performance in the aspect in which you are feeling incompetent.

✓ Undertake training.

✓ Start reading about the subject.

✓ Learn and grow.

✓ One in five people tend to be perfectionists and will need to challenge their criteria and check whether the expectations they set for themself are realistic and achievable.

✓ Use the opportunity to be the powerful YOU.

e. Grief and Loss

Losing someone or something that is valuable to you and grieving this loss is a natural part of life. Everyone experiences these feelings differently, but there are coping techniques that you can use to make this time a time of healing.

The message:

> ✓ *You have lost someone or something valuable to you*

The action required:

✓ Tell yourself the quickest way through grief is to go slow.

✓ Allow yourself to feel the feeling – allow yourself to come to terms with what has happened .

✓ Move through the stages of grief (indicated in diagram below).

✓ If you are really struggling, consult your GP/Medical Practitioner.

✓ Live in celebration of a passed loved one's life, not in the sadness of their death.

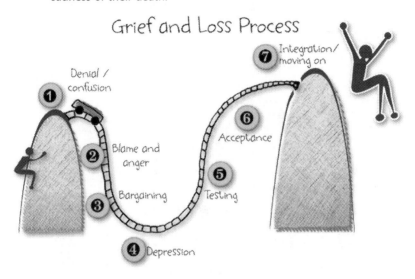

Grief and Loss Process

Quick Reference Guide

The following table is a quick reference guide to most of the common unpleasant emotions you may experience. Please refer to this section often, it will assist you to understand the messages your unpleasant emotions are conveying, and suggest actions for you to take in response.

Remember, you have a responsibility to feel good; so listen to the message and take the action required to move beyond your unpleasant emotional experience and return to feeling good.

Please note: You may or may not identify with one or many of the messages indicated. At different times and in different situations, you will find different messages and actions applicable. However, regardless of how many you relate to at any given moment, it is essential to identify what your emotions are, the messages they convey and the necessary actions to take.

Emotion	Message	What Action To Take
Anger	• The desire, need or expectation you have is not being met • A standard or rule you have set for yourself was or is violated either by you or someone else • Someone has hurt you and you have not expressed the hurt you feel	• Change your expectations • Put the issue into perspective • Step into the shoes of the other person • Express yourself assertively and constructively to influence the change you are passionate about
Anxiety	• You think/feel something bad might happen that you will not be able or willing to cope with. • It is a response to a real, imagined or anticipated change in your environment	• Get ready and prepare for the anticipated event • Focus and figure out how to deal with the change • Recall the reality that most things you have been anxious about never happen • Relax and take action • Do breathing exercises. Example: breathe in for ten seconds, hold for five seconds and breathe out for ten seconds. All the while, focus entirely on your breathing

Emotion	Message	What Action To Take
Bitterness and jealousy	• You feel as if someone you trusted has betrayed you • You regularly think that life has not delivered what you think you deserve • You feel that someone or something else is getting the attention, time, money or other resources that you want to have	• Tell yourself you can influence, but not control others • Forgive, let go and be free (See chapter 9) • Improve your own ability to attract the attention, time, money, or other resources that you desire in your life • Cultivate feelings of gratitude and by focussing your attention on what you have • Jealousy in relationships: Ensure that you are more pleasant and attractive to be with than anybody else • Improve yourself and your own self-esteem by applying the methods outlined in this book
Feeling mildly depressed Note: If you are feeling severely depressed, please consult your General Practitioner as soon as possible	• You are withdrawing from others • Your thinking-feeling addiction is negative and rapidly spiralling downward • An expectation you have has not been met • A need you have has not been met • You are feeling overwhelmed and fearful (refer to overloaded and overwhelmed, and fear and worry to see appropriate action to take)	• Do something: act into a new way of thinking • Use the process outlined in chapter 6 to create a positive thinking-feeling addiction • Talk back positively to yourself • Challenge your thoughts • Foster gratitude • Take action • Change your expectations

Emotion	Message	What Action To Take
Disappoint-ment	• You have an expectation or need that has not been or is yet to be met	• Use your conscious mind to examine what your expectation or need is • Consider whether your expectation is/was realistic • Examine whether you need to attempt a different approach in order for the expectation to be met or the need fulfilled • Determine if there is a lesson to be learnt about another person: are they showing you who they really are and should you take the feedback on board?
Doubt	• You are progressing into an area that is unfamiliar to you	• Clarify your Goals • Does this new direction take you closer to your goals? • If 'YES', you are on the right track - progress in spite of the doubt – the doubt is a normal part of any new venture • If 'NO', take a different course of action that will lead you the achievement of your goals • If 'MAYBE', then progress with your course of action to give yourself the opportunity to get more feedback to be able to make an informed decision • Doubt is a natural feeling when you are embarking on a new venture, changing direction or moving into a place you have not been before • Feel the doubt and do it anyway
• Embarrass-ment	• You feel as though you are being noticed or stand out for a negative reason	• Maximise your positive attributes and strengths • Learn to accept and love yourself • Learn from and let go of past failures • Choose to feel good • Be grateful for what you have

Emotion	Message	What Action To Take
• Fear and worry	• You are facing a perceived threat or risk • Get ready and prepare	• Define the risk or threat • Determine the ideal outcome • Consider if it is really a risk or threat • Set a plan of action in place to overcome or avoid the risk/threat • Implement your plan • Do everything possible and trust God to do the impossible • Foster an expectation that all will work out well
• Feelings of failure	• You have a lesson to learn • If you have tried something that has not worked, there is valuable feedback you will need to take on board • If you learn the lesson now, you will never have to go through the same process again • It is only a failure if you fail to learn the lesson	• Feel encouraged that you have tried something, even though it has not worked out the way you intended. However, you are one step closer to achieving what you wanted if you learn the lesson and try again • No failure can 'stop' you - only you can 'stop' you • Learn and apply the lesson • Use your mind and be creative in finding a different approach • Keep going/moving boldly in the direction of your aim
Frustration	• What you are doing is not working • Try a different approach • Try a different course of action	• Clearly define what you are trying to achieve • Be flexible, resourceful and creative in finding the various approaches to achieve the same goal • Stop doing what you are doing right now • Attempt a different way or approach

Emotion	Message	What Action To Take
Grief and loss	• You have lost someone or something valuable to you	• See your GP/Medical Practitioner if you are really struggling • Tell yourself the quickest way through grief is to go slow • Allow yourself to feel the feeling – allow yourself to come to terms with what has happened • Move through the stages of grief (as outlined in the diagram in the grief and loss section before this table) • Live in celebration of a passed loved one's life, not in the sadness of their death
Guilt and regret	• You have violated a standard you have set for yourself • You have not lived up to the expectations you have of yourself • You have broken a rule that you set in life	• Ask for forgiveness • Remedy the situation if possible • Set a goal to learn from this experience and not repeat it • Forgive yourself • Relax. Review your expectations. How realistic are they?
Hate	• A need you have has not been met • A boundary you have set in your life has been acutely violated • The rules that have been set for yourself and your life have been broken • An acute amount of unexpressed hurt has built up	• Consider what advantage it is for you to maintain your rage • Who is benefiting from your reaction? • Let go (See chapter 8 for how)

Emotion	Message	What Action To Take
Insecurity and inadequacy	• You have to grow and improve yourself and/or your skills • The standards by which you measure yourself/the expectations you set for yourself are too high	• Use your conscious mind to examine the situation • Determine what area in which you need to improve/grow • Devise a growth or improvement plan for yourself • Look for resources like books, courses and other people to assist you with the improvements you need to make • Start improving immediately • Consider the standards you have set for yourself – are they stretching but achievable? If not, use your conscious mind to consider different standards that will allow you to succeed and feel good about yourself
Loneliness	• You need to build a relationship with another person • You have to reach out to another person • You have a need for a relationship with another human being • You have love to share with someone • You must connect with someone	• Clarify in your mind the relationship you need • You have to give, in order to get • Enter the area of action where you will find the type of people you need to connect with • Reach out and give friendship, love and care first and you will receive the same in return

Emotion	Message	What Action To Take
Overloaded and over-whelmed	• You do not have a clear and work-able action plan of what, how, when and by whom something needs to be done • You are taking on too much at one time	• Make a master list of all you need to do and what you are concerned about • Divide the list into two sections: 1. Things you can and must do 2. Things you cannot actively improve or change • Write a to-do list. Prioritise and delegate if possible • Schedule time and deadlines for all other tasks • Take action! Just do it! • Vigorous exercise will rid your body of built up tension • Foster an optimistic expectation that all will turn out well • Learn to say NO • Schedule time to rest and relax
Rejection and hurt	• An expectation you have has not been met • Your emotional response to someone's actions • A need you have has not been met	• Examine your needs and expectations • Ask, 'Am I being over sensitive?' • What you are feeling might not be about you, but rather an indication of who the other person is • Take the feedback and adjust your behaviour if necessary

Emotion	Message	What Action To Take
Stress	• Your passion for life is being smothered • You are allowing some things to become more important than they really are • You are allowing a foundation of fear to produce stress and skepticism in your life • You are losing perspective	• A limited level of stress is a good thing • Repeat the question, 'Is this worth losing my health over?' • Cultivate a positive perspective about the future • Act your way out of stress and into a calmer position by employing the strategy outlined in 'overloaded and overwhelmed' • Undertake moderate exercise
Upset	• Relates to your expectation of other people and how they should behave or act towards you or something you care about	• Remember you cannot control other people, you can only control you • You teach people how to treat you • Examine your expectations of the other person • Accept this person for who they are in the present • Examine if you should allow yourself to be involved with this person • Communicate your expectations clearly • Consider how you can serve that person first without any expectations

Every emotional experience you have is valuable. Ensure you experience the feel-good emotions 90 percent of your life and use the remaining 10 percent of unpleasant emotional experiences to your benefit. Allow them to help you grow, improve and learn as much as possible.

CHAPTER 9

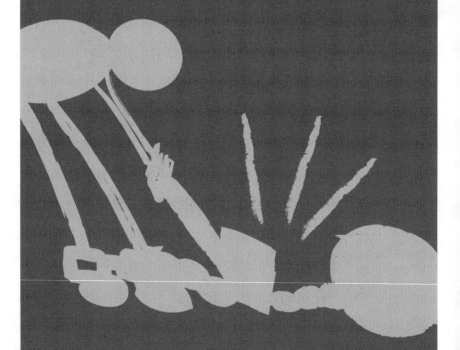

Smash Your Shackles

Getting hurt and being violated or offended by others is an unavoidable part of being human.

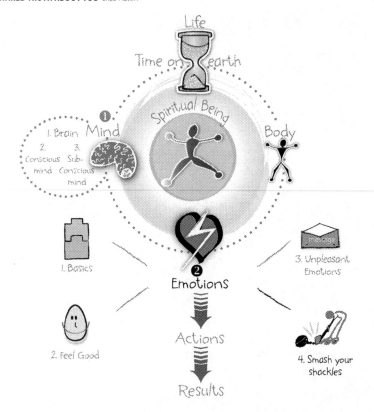

Getting hurt and being violated or offended by others is an unavoidable part of being human. It may also be assumed that you, in turn, will intentionally or unintentionally offend, hurt or violate others. These experiences, however difficult to endure, create opportunities for you to grow in strength and power. When they are handled correctly, you can draw enormous strength from overcoming this inevitable aspect of your human experience.

What are shackles?

Getting hurt is unavoidable, but your corresponding emotional response is optional. Many people harbour feelings of anger, resentment, bitterness and disappointment in their hearts and minds. These feelings fester and grow with time, acting as Shackles. Shackles are negative emotional responses to past hurtful experiences. Shackles become impossibly heavy, holding you back and tying you down. Shackles drag you down, slow you down and prevent you from achieving your full potential.

However, there is a way to break the shackles currently holding you back. There is a way to let go, move on and be free to live your best life. Too many people alive today are not living an extraordinary life because past experiences of hurt and offence hold them back. Do not allow yourself to be one of these people. As long as you have shackles dragging you down, you are not free to live well. The key to breaking your shackles is forgiveness.

What forgiveness is *not!*

The common misconception of forgiveness is that when you forgive, you condone the offender's behaviour. Forgiving someone does not make what they did right, nor does it mean you accept or advocate their actions.

Think about this for a moment. The people who have offended and hurt you in the past are probably living their lives reasonably unaffected by the grudge you hold towards them. However, your life is still very much affected by the shackles created as a result of their past behaviour - their past actions are still influencing your present life. Consequently, forgiveness has nothing to do with the perpetrators and offenders; it is all about you. Forgiveness is breaking the shackles and setting you free!

Why should you forgive?

Forgiveness allows you to be set free from the perpetrator's control over you. By forgiving, you regain personal control; you no longer allow past hurts to negatively affect your present life. Remember, your perpetrators are getting on with their own lives anyway. Their lives are not affected by the fact you have not forgiven them, but your life is being affected significantly as you continue to hold on to these shackles. So, let go! Forgiveness is your key to freedom.

Forgiveness is:

- ✓ A choice only you can make.
- ✓ This choice will only benefit you.
- ✓ Not forgiving results in you living a life of oppression.
- ✓ While you carry resentment in your heart and mind, you allow the offender's actions to control and affect you daily.
- ✓ Forgiving sets you free.

Forgiving yourself

Forgiveness is generally related to the wrongs others have done to you. However, bitterness can develop in your life as a result of you feeling hurt and regret from the wrong doings you have committed towards others. Just as you hurt from being hurt, you also hurt from hurting others. After all, hurting people hurts people.

If you hold on to hurt and refuse to forgive yourself, you create a vicious cycle that is draining and highly difficult to break free of. As a result, you continue to hurt others, even when you do not intend to.

Therefore, when you make a mistake or do wrong by other people, you must let go of your past mistakes by forgiving yourself. As stated previously, whether you intend to or not, you will hurt someone at least once in your lifetime. Even if you intentionally hurt someone in the past, it is of no benefit to you to hold on to that regret and hurt that is destroying your life. Instead, forgive yourself and if possible seek forgiveness from those whom you have hurt or violated and be free.

How do you forgive?

Now you are ready to smash your shackles and set yourself free by forgiving, the work begins. The strength of the shackles depends on the length of time and the severity of the hurt, bitterness and resentment carried within you. The stronger your shackles, the harder you will have to work to break free. Nevertheless, your freedom will be well worth the effort.

There is no quick fix to forgiveness. Only you have the power to forgive, as no one can force you to forgive another. Unfortunately, it is sometimes not an easy path to tread. Forgiveness is an active step-by-step process. Your first step is realising you want your future to be better than your past.

Think of forgiveness as making a declaration for a better future - letting go of the past in order to move on. In forgiving the past, you set yourself free; setting yourself up to succeed in the future.

As soon as you have made the decision to forgive, it is time to take action. Remember, this is a process and some steps may bring up the past emotions which caused you harm. Please consult a psychologist or counsellor if you require assistance in this process. Think of this process as a life detoxification and, just like after having a physical detox, you will be healthier than you were before.

7 Steps to smashing your shackles

Step 1.   Compile a list of names of people who have hurt you in the past, or individuals towards whom you feel resentment or hold a grudge against.

Step 2.   Compile and write out a list of people and their actions who you have decided to forgive. Use a forgiveness journal; it can be any book, but is a special book that you will destroy at the end of this process.

Step 3.   At the top of the page write: "I forgive (the person's name) for (what he/she has done to hurt me)" and journal your feelings about this person and the hurt that has been caused.

Step 4.   Repeat Step 3 until you have listed all the individuals and wrongs for which you need to forgive.

Step 5.   Upon completion of the list, speak these sentences out loud: *"I forgive (the person's name) for (what he/she has done to hurt me)".* By speaking them out loud, you declare not only to yourself, but also to the world that you are letting go and smashing your shackles.

Step 6.   Destroy your forgiveness journal as a sign you have forgiven and let go of the resentment you have felt in the past.

Step 7.   Whenever emotions or thoughts of resentment return, repeat the following sentence as a declaration of and commitment to your forgiveness: *"I have forgiven (person's name) and I am free."* Repeat this as many times as necessary.

Your shackles prevent you from being the best and powerful YOU and living a celebrated life. Engage actively in the process of forgiveness, thus smashing the shackles that drag you down. Your bonus for working through this process will be the strength you gain from overcoming past hurtful experiences. You will grow in strength throughout this process, and this strength will accompany you into your extraordinary life.

CHAPTER 10

Master Your Body

YOU have been given a
magnificent tool – a remarkable
feat of engineering and an
incredible masterpiece.

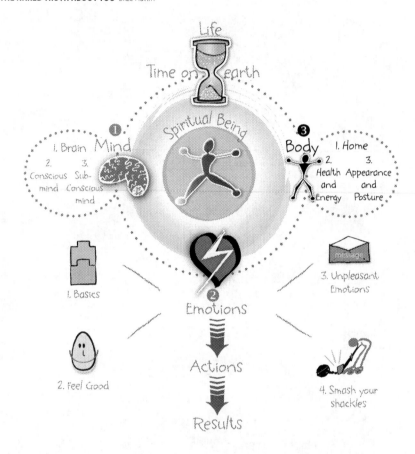

Your body is a masterpiece

YOU have been given a magnificent tool – a remarkable feat of engineering and an incredible masterpiece. This tool is able to do much more than the most expensive and advanced technology available. This tool is capable of conceiving and giving birth to a child, running a marathon, holding a feather and throwing a stone. This tool is capable of walking, jumping, speaking and singing. This amazing tool is your body.

Your body is a wonder:

✓ Your thigh bone is the strongest bone in your body, in fact, it is stronger than concrete... and is hollow.

✓ Your lungs contain over 300,000 million tiny blood vessels (capillaries). If they were laid end to end, they would stretch 2,400km (1,500 miles).

✓ On average, your heart will beat approximately 3 billion times in your lifetime.

✓ Your focussing muscles in your eyes move around 100,000 times a day.

✓ Each square inch of your skin contains twenty feet of blood vessels.

✓ Your skeleton consists of 213 bones.

✓ Your body contains more than 600 individual skeletal muscles.

✓ Your skin contains approximately 640,000 sense receptors.

✓ Your adult human body contains approximately 100 trillion cells.

✓ You have about 60 muscles in your face. Smiling is easier than frowning, as smiling only requires the use of 20 muscles and frowning requires over 40.

Your body is the home for YOU as a spiritual being

While bricks and mortar have built your physical home, your body is YOUR Spiritual Being's home. It becomes YOUR palace and temple for the time YOU live on earth. YOU only have one chance to live on earth as a human being. Therefore, YOU will only have one body in which to experience life on earth.

Are you taking your body for granted? Have you become dissatisfied with the amazing body you have been given? Are you mistreating your home? Are you abusing your palace?

YOU will only receive one body. Appreciating, respecting and loving your body is essential for getting the best from it and gaining the most from your life on earth.

Who is in control: YOU or your body?

YOU are a Spiritual Being having a human experience. Your body is your vessel, the human home that YOU, as a Spiritual Being, inhabit while living on earth. YOU have been given this body, enabling YOU to spend time on earth as a human being. The body YOU have been given is your vehicle, carrying YOU through the many stages of your human life experience.

Unfortunately, many people allow their bodies to be in control. However, when YOU learn to master, control and love your body, your life will improve significantly. In your quest to 'overcome' your body, you will learn how to love, respect, manage and make use of it as your precious home. The function of your conscious mind, Will (chapter 4), is your essential tool in mastering your body. Be strong willed about loving and caring for YOUR home.

You require high levels of health and energy

Action fuels results! To achieve extraordinary results in life, you are required to take action. Your body is the tool that enables YOU to take this action. Just as your car needs petrol to run, you also need high levels of health and energy! To feel energetic, empowered, productive and positive, YOU must take care of your body and ensure you have high levels of health and energy, thus supporting the actions required to live an extraordinary life. With high levels of health and energy, you will feel empowered and productive, resulting in wealthy living!

So what to do...

Every day we are bombarded with ways to improve our health. Television shows are even dedicated to the cause, yet there are still those who continue to ignore the warnings. This is especially frightening when considering the fact that people living in the western world are among the most well informed people on earth when it comes to caring for their bodies.

By taking care of your body, YOU are inadvertently caring for your spirit also. Good health and energy is essential for living an extraordinary life. Prioritising the following nine simple strategies will ensure you achieve and maintain good physical health.

1. Healthy nutrition.

2. Moderate weight-bearing and cardiovascular exercise.

3. Dietary supplements.

4. Adequate daily water intake.

5. Quality sleep.

6. Breathing well.

7. Good oral hygiene.

8. Adequate rest and relaxation.

9. Regular health checkups with your health professional and taking immediate action with any health challenges that may arise.

Please note: This is not a dedicated health and exercise book, so please seek further information about specific health-related topics if required.

Health is YOUR choice

Imagine yourself sitting at a roundabout. You have a decision to make: Do you go straight through, left or right? Whichever direction you choose will alter your path, taking you to a completely different destination. This same principle applies to how you look after your body.

Every morning when you get out of bed, you sit at a crossroads. YOU can choose how YOU will treat your body during that day. The choices YOU make daily determine YOUR body's 'destination' – its overall health and energy. YOU should make a conscious decision to treat your body well every day! Your ultimate health depends on the choices you make in the 'now', the present moment of every day. So, choose health every time you buy your food. Choose health by choosing to prepare healthy, nutritious meals. Choose health by incorporating movement into your day. Choose to take the stairs, choose to walk to work and choose to dance when the music plays. Good health is the result of consistent daily healthy choices made over time. Always choose health!

By making good choices, you ensure your body, the vessel that carries YOUR spirit, can bear you through your extraordinary life here on earth.

Check your subconscious programming

Ask yourself, 'Are any of my health challenges the result of a bad subconscious program?'

As discussed in chapter 5, you will always behave in a manner consistent with your subconscious programming. For example, Jane struggles with being over-weight. She successfully loses weight by following a diet, only to regain the weight once the diet stops. Jane has a bad program running in her subconscious mind that says, 'I AM FAT!' Jane constantly reinforces this bad program by saying, 'I don't want to be fat, why am I so fat?' as well as telling herself not to be fat. Jane's bad subconscious program will guarantee she will always be overweight, as she is unable to behave in a manner inconsistent with her programming.

Examples of bad health programming include:

      ×   I am fat.

      ×   I hate exercise.

      ×   I am weak.

      ×   I am sick/always sick.

      ×   I don't want to get sick.

      ×   I am tired.

      ×   I am stressed.

Replacing the bad programs with these good programs, through the process outlined in chapter 5, will ensure being healthy is easy and sustainable. These good programs include:

      ✓   I can eat whatever I want and always maintain
          the perfect weight.

      ✓   I am healthy.

✓ I am strong.

✓ I am well.

✓ I am energetic.

✓ I am attractive.

✓ I am confident.

✓ I am friendly.

✓ I am happy.

✓ I feel good.

✓ I choose health daily.

✓ I love using my body.

✓ My body enjoys moving.

✓ My body enjoys exercise.

✓ I love my body.

✓ I care for my body.

Emotions cause actions, actions determine results

As discussed in chapter 6, your emotions cause you to act. Therefore it is fair to say that if you are struggling with your weight there will be an unpleasant emotion you are trying to deal with or avoid by distracting yourself with food and eating. Apply your conscious mind to analyse your feelings when you eat or want to eat. Be mindful of the emotions you experience that cause you to use food as a distraction. Food and eating will never allow you to overcome your unpleasant emotions. If you are dealing with your unpleasant emotions by eating, you are preventing yourself from living an extraordinary life. Overeating will only result in more unpleasant emotions, creating a negative spiral. Your unpleasant emotions are trying to teach you something about yourself or your life (chapter 8). For example, if you are eating to avoid listening to and deal-ing with feelings of loneliness, you are preventing yourself from making new friends, connecting with new people and contributing your unique gifts to the world around you. If you are overeating due to feelings of frustration, you are preventing yourself from growing and improving by trying a different way.

If you find you overeat (or experience any other eating challenges) to deal with unpleasant emotions, here is what you can do to improve your life: Define the unpleasant emotion and listen to the message by doing one, two or all of the following:

- Reprogram your subconscious mind with good programs (chapter 5).

- Smash the shackles that are holding you back and causing you to overeat (chapter 9).

- Heed the message about yourself or your life by using the process outlined in chapter 8.

Changing your posture will change your life

As discussed in chapter 5, your emotions are the link between your mind and your body. Your thoughts affect your feelings and your feelings affect your body. The opposite is true too! Your body affects your feelings and your feelings affect your thoughts.

For example, when you feel happy, you smile. Conversely, if you purposefully start smiling when you feel unhappy, your emotions will adjust to your smile and you will feel better. Your emotions adjust according to your body language and posture. By consciously adopting the body language of happy, confident and successful people, you will start to feel more happy, confident and successful. How you feel drives your action and your action fuels the results of your life. Just imagine what you will achieve when you feel happy, confident and attractive! Adjusting your body language will change your life!

Other people also engage with you according to your body language and posture. Body language constitutes more than 50% of what you communicate about yourself to the world. It is through the use of your body language and posture that others decide how to respond to you. Other people respond according to what you are communicating to them with your posture. What an opportunity. YOU can master and control your body language!

Engage your conscious mind and control your body. Use the strength of your will to stand, sit and use your body in a manner consistent with your desired

feelings. By consciously maintaining the best posture or body language, you will be able to affect how others perceive you and more importantly, how you feel about yourself. Over time, your body will adjust to and accept this new successful body language and posture.

To foster a happy and confident body posture:

- Stand up straight and tall.

- Always keep your arms uncrossed. The moment you cross your arms, you close your mind to new ideas.

- Keep arms and legs uncrossed when seated. Keep your body open! (You might feel vulnerable initially, but stick with it. You will start feeling more confident soon).

- Keep your chin up.

- Smile.

- Establish and maintain eye contact with other people.

- Animate your face when talking.

- Keep your palms open – it shows honesty and makes others feel more comfortable in your presence.

- Keep your fingers together – this shows you are competent and knowledgeable.

- Maintain a pleasant and happy expression on your face.

Actively creating confidence, happiness and attractiveness from the outside, via body language and posture, will bring about positive emotional changes on the inside, making you feel better. Adopting these body postures will enable you to feel good and allow others to see you as being more attractive and confident.

Note: studying body language will empower you to adjust your body posture to create your desired emotions and image.

Dress for success...

Have you noticed that how you feel influences what you wear? Conversely, what you wear will influence the way you feel. As people scrutinise your appearance, they acquire a sense of who you are.

Take care in your appearance. Be disciplined in wearing only the clothing, styles and colours that portray you at your best. Dress appropriately for every occasion. Dressing well does not have to be expensive. The price tag on clothing does not indicate the value of the person wearing the clothing. Enjoy and celebrate your body by wearing clothes that make you feel alive and well.

Simple grooming, hygiene, hair care and make-up are essential when it comes to caring for and loving your body. It is your responsibility to respect your body and care for it on every level.

When you care for this magnificent tool you have been equipped with, it will, in turn, care for YOU. A healthy body will help you achieve everything you desire – and more. Additionally, when you feel healthy and attractive, you are confident, so make the effort daily to look after your body in every way possible, enabling you to take on everything that comes your way. Make a conscious effort to look after your one and only body and appreciate it for all it is worth!

CHAPTER 11

Live Your Unique Extraordinary Life

Your life is a gift.
This prized gift of your life
allows YOU the opportunity to
spend time on earth. YOU, as
a Spiritual Being, have been
given this human life to live.

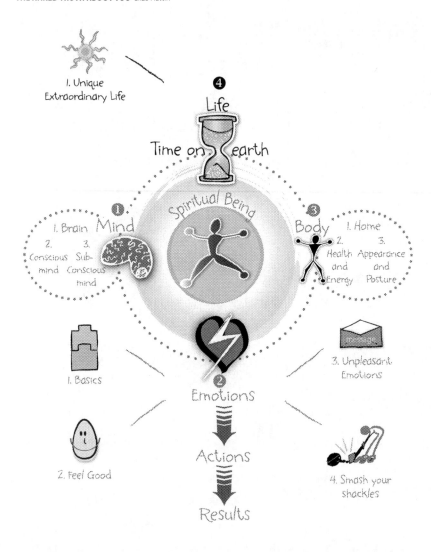

This prized gift of your life allows YOU the opportunity to spend time on earth. YOU, as a Spiritual Being, have been given this human life to live. However, YOU will only receive one life; therefore this is your sole opportunity to experience its wonder. As a result, it is your responsibility to care for and value this gift you have been given.

Your life is measured in the unit of time

Your life on earth is measured in seconds, minutes, hours, days, weeks, months, years and decades. Each year brings a commemoration of your time spent on earth - your birthday.

However, as a Spiritual Being, your existence is not governed by your human form. YOU as a Spiritual Being exist beyond your human life. After your time on earth has ended, YOU will continue to exist in spiritual form forever. This is in contrast to your human existence, which is very much bound and limited by time. As a Spiritual Being, YOU are immortal, yet your time on earth is limited with a specific beginning (your conception) and a specific end (your death). Value your time on earth; you will not be here forever.

Your life is significant and important

Your existence is not random, nor is it a fluke. You exist at this time for a reason and have a significant and valuable contribution to make to your community and the world. Your life is important!

You are fighting to stay alive every day. You would not keep up the fight for survival if you did not have a deep understanding that your life is important. Your life is important to you, your family, your community and the world, so live your life as if it is important! Make your life count!

You have work to do – your life's work

You were born into this world for a reason. You have your Life's Work to do. Your Life's Work is defined as using your unique gifts, talents and abilities in your field of interest to fulfil a need in the world. In short, your Life's Work is: improving your environment by doing what you love. A need exists in the world that you were born to fulfil. You were born for a specific purpose and there are people depending on you to do your Life's Work. As you look around at the world in which you live, you will see much need. Need exists because many people are not engaged in their Life's Work.

Only you can do your Life's Work. If you do not find and engage in your Life's Work, it will sadly remain undone and the need will linger in the world. It is your responsibility to uncover and engage in your Life's Work, improving your world by doing what you love.

You can (and should) choose to enjoy your life

Your life offers you a choice. You can either choose to:

1. Enjoy your life and take full advantage of every opportunity your life offers; or

2. You can choose to lead an unhappy life whilst complaining and blaming others for your lack of enjoyment.

This decision is yours to make; no one can make it for you. Do not waste another day waiting for someone else to make your life better - it is just not going to happen. Do not waste another day waiting for the people around you to change so you can be happy. You cannot control other people, you can only control yourself. Expecting others to make you happy or blaming others for the lack of enjoyment of your own life is giving your power and control over yourself away; allowing others to control the enjoyment of your life. Take responsibility for your own life as it is in this very moment and choose to lead an extraordinary life.

Living a great life is not any harder than living a dull and unpleasant life - yet it is so much more enjoyable and fun. You have both versions of life available, however it is up to you to choose the good life, take responsibility for yourself and your life, and make it happen.

When is your life?

You will always live and experience your life in the 'now', the present moment. Yesterday is past and tomorrow never comes; your life is now! Every second is equally important and gives you equal opportunity to experience your gift of life.

Many people live in the past or the future mentally. This prevents them from being present, mindful and enjoying their lives in the moment - in the now. The only time that is and will ever be in existence, is now.

It is essential to look back at the things you have done and learn from the past. Learning from the past will enable you to create a brighter future. It is also essential to dream about and plan for your future. However, you should focus on living your life in the present.

Your future's circumstances will depend on the actions you take in the present. Results always lag behind activity. When you get to the future, you will still be experiencing those results in the 'now'. So live mindfully in the present and plan for the future. Be conscious of the activities you do in the present, understanding that you are creating your own future.

Eleanor Roosevelt said rightly that:

> *"Yesterday is History,*
> *Tomorrow is a Mystery,*
> *Today is a Gift,*
> *That's why it's called the Present"*

Don't let your life pass you by without ever being *present*.

Your life has seasons – there is a time for everything!

Just like the seasons within nature – spring giving way to summer and autumn making way for winter – so your life also progresses through seasons or stages. One season or stage seamlessly melds with the next.

Every person has the opportunity to experience each human season once. We all have the same opportunity to live life as a baby, young child, teenager, young adult, adult and an elderly member of the community. Each season offers something new to learn and experience. Each season is special and important. As you pass through each season, you will notice that your goals change. The goals you set for yourself as a teenager are probably remarkably different to the goals you set as an adult. Just as you grow and mature physically, what you want from life will grow and mature with you.

Erik Erikson was a psychologist who described the developments that occur throughout a person's life. The table below will give you insight into the eight stages of your life as well as the goals and relationships of each stage.

Life Stage	Theme	What you hope to achieve	Important Relationships
Infant	Feeding, being comforted, teething, sleeping	Hope and Drive	Mother
Toddler	Bodily functions, toilet training, muscular control, walking	Willpower and Self-Control	Parents
Preschool	Exploration, discovery, adventure and play	Purpose and Direction	Family
Schoolchild	Achievement and accomplishment	Competence and Method	School, teachers, friends, neighbourhood
Adolescent	Resolving identity and direction, becoming a grown-up	Fidelity and Devotion	Peers, groups, social influences
Young adult	Intimate relationships, work and social life	Love and Affiliation	Lovers, friends, work connections
Mid-adult	'Giving back', helping, contributing	Care and Production	Children, community
Late adult	Meaning and purpose, life achievements	Wisdom and Renunciation	Society, the world, life

There is always something great to enjoy in each of the natural seasons. Winter brings afternoons snuggled under a blanket in front of the fire reading a book; spring is about new life and warm days; summer calls you to spend time enjoying a walk along the beach at sunset; and autumn reveals wonderful colours and flavours that overflow into your cooking. The same applies to the seasons of your life. Enjoy living in the present season and appreciate the great things associated with it. Every life stage is special and meaningful. While it is perfectly normal to plan for the next season, don't forget to live in the present. Make the most of the season you are in. Otherwise, it will pass by before you truly have a chance to enjoy it!

ALL THE WORLD'S A STAGE
(FROM AS YOU LIKE IT 2/7)

All the world's a stage,
And all the men and women merely players:
They have their exits and their entrances;
And one man in his time plays many parts,
His acts being seven ages. At first the infant,
Mewling and puking in the nurse's arms.
And then the whining school-boy, with his satchel
And shining morning face, creeping like snail
Unwillingly to school. And then the lover,
Sighing like furnace, with a woeful ballad
Made to his mistress' eyebrow. Then a soldier,
Full of strange oaths and bearded like the pard,
Jealous in honour, sudden and quick in quarrel,
Seeking the bubble reputation
Even in the cannon's mouth. And then the justice,
In fair round belly with good capon lined,
With eyes severe and beard of formal cut,
Full of wise saws and modern instances;
And so he plays his part. The sixth age shifts
Into the lean and slipper'd pantaloon,
With spectacles on nose and pouch on side,
His youthful hose, well saved, a world too wide
For his shrunk shank; and his big manly voice,
Turning again toward childish treble, pipes
And whistles in his sound. Last scene of all,
That ends this strange eventful history,
Is second childishness and mere oblivion,
Sans teeth, sans eyes, sans taste, sans everything.

WILLIAM SHAKESPEARE

How many hats do you wear?
Do you have several identities?

There are several sides or facets to who you are. Each version is a slightly different facet of you. Do you relate to your mother and your spouse in the same manner? More than likely not. You will never relate to your children in the same way you relate to your employer; you wear different hats and play different roles daily.

As you engage and interact with different people and environments, you will behave differently. You would not engage or behave in the same manner with your friends as you would with your children. Additionally, you would not behave in the same manner with your partner as with your parents. Depending on where you are and with whom you interact, you have the ability to automatically select the appropriate role needed for the situation. Each of your identities highlights a facet of who you are.

However, each identity is important and must be developed for you to live your extraordinary life. As a result, you must work to develop and grow each of your identities to be the best you can be.

Take a moment to write down all of the identities you have in your life. Think about each one consciously and deliberately, and decide who you want to be in each role you play. Then, be the best self, parent, partner, colleague, employee, neighbour, friend, sibling, child or boss you can be!

Aspects of your life...

Your life is divided into different aspects. These aspects signify all the different sections of your life which are important to you and together constitute your whole life. Consider your life as a wheel. This wheel is divided into different segments, representing different aspects of your life. The universally important aspects are health, wealth, career, family, friends and other relationships, your home and physical environment, spirituality, contribution, etc.

Aspects of your Life

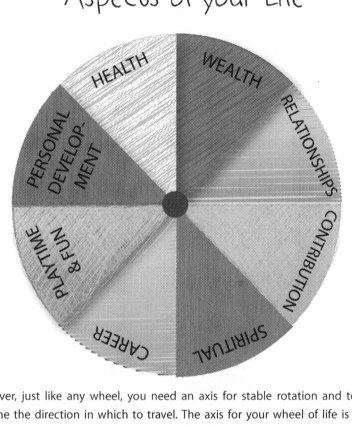

However, just like any wheel, you need an axis for stable rotation and to determine the direction in which to travel. The axis for your wheel of life is your subconscious mind's programming combined with your values, as discussed in chapter 5. You will always behave in a manner consistent with your programs. These programs are extremely powerful in directing the way you live your life.

Engage in every aspect of your life consciously, mindfully, deliberately and intentionally. It is also important to set goals for every aspect of your life, enabling you to work towards what you want, as well as ensuring your programming is keeping your wheel stable.

Balance is everything!

You are constantly bombarded with the fact that it is necessary to have a balanced diet by eating the right food in the correct proportions. This same principle applies to your life. You must ensure all aspects of your life are in balance and in the correct proportions. Without the correct balance in the aspects of your life, your wheel will start to wear and become unsafe. For example, if a businessman spends too much time in the office, working all hours away from his wife and family, his relationships with his wife and family will suffer – it becomes unbalanced. The businessman runs the risk of losing not only his wife and family, but also his work, as his life is not in balance or proportion.

As a result of taking care and responsibility for your wheel, ensuring every aspect of your life is balanced, your wheel will run smoothly for the rest of your life. A well-maintained wheel of life will ensure you do not miss out on any aspect of the extraordinary life that is yours for the living.

Your extraordinary life

Do you entertain thoughts of an extraordinary life? How does it look, feel and sound? Every person is unique and, therefore, every extraordinary life is uniquely different. Most people spend more time and resources planning a vacation than they will ever spend thinking about and planning their own lives. What a missed opportunity!

How to create an extraordinary life

By thinking through and defining the time, aspects, stages of your life, the identities you hold and how to balance it all, you will create your own unique extraordinary life. Your extraordinary life - unique and designed completely by you.

The process to achieve this unique extraordinary life is so simple that anyone can do it. It is not only simple, but highly effective and successful as well.

The first and very important step is to acquire a folder to keep next to your bed. This folder will contain the images, words and thoughts that describe and represent your extraordinary life. By reading through this folder first thing in the morning, you are programming your subconscious mind to realise your extraordinary life.

You are only required to make two commitments to ensure your extraordinary life; it's as easy as that!

1. Define your extraordinary life on paper. Compile your extraordinary life folder with words, personal power statement, pictures, images, poems, photographs, etc.

2. Spend five minutes reading through your folder first thing in the morning, before you get out of bed. This will create new programs in your subconscious mind. These programs will over time enable you to perform the actions required to create your extraordinary life.

How to define your extraordinary life:

Answering the following questions will start you on the process of designing your extraordinary life. Remember, there is no right or wrong answer. Just write down what comes to mind and go with your intuition. It is your life to live and your life to design. Perfection is not the goal, extraordinary is the aim. Define your own unique extraordinary life in your own unique way.

13 Questions every person should answer about and for their life!

1. What would my extraordinary life look, feel, sound, taste and smell like?

2. What do I dream of achieving in my lifetime?

3. What is my ideal daily routine?

4. What would I like to say that I truly know, in my life and about my life?

5. What identities do I hold and how can I be the best me in every role?

6. How would I like to relate to other people? My family, my friends, my colleagues, my community?

7. What would I like other people to think about me?

8. What emotions would I like to experience during my life-time?

9. What aspects of my life are important and what do I want to do, feel, experience and achieve in each aspect?

10. What is it that I would like to be doing in two years time? Five years? Ten years? Twenty years? At the end of my life?

11. What does balance look, feel and sound like for my life?

12. What would I like to learn during my lifetime?

13. Who would I like to become during my lifetime? What character would I like to develop during my lifetime?

Answer these questions and record your answers in your Extraordinary Life folder, along with any pictures, words, items, etc. that inspire you to live your unique extraordinary life. To gain maximum benefit from this exercise, it is beneficial for you to review your answers daily.

Engage in your life consciously and deliberately. Think about your life and the time you have to spend. Design your life. Plan the life you want to live and most importantly, make the most of the time you have on earth. Remember, you only get to live life once, so being mindful and engaging in your life consciously is the first step towards living an extraordinary life.

CHAPTER 12

Make the Most of Time

Your life is measured in, governed and bound by time. Your human experience has a specific beginning (your conception) and a specific end (your death).

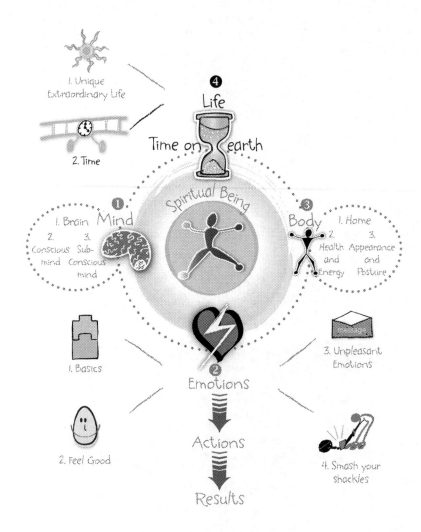

The unit your life is measured in is TIME...

Your life is measured in, governed and bound by time. Your human experience has a specific beginning (your conception) and a specific end (your death). However, as a Spiritual Being, YOU are timeless and immortal and will continue to exist after your human experience ends.

Since your time on earth is limited, time is one of your most valuable assets. Time is one of the resources available to you that can never be replaced or regained once it has passed. Money lost can be recouped, even possessions once lost can be replaced, but your time on earth is irreplaceable. Therefore, it is vital to spend your time wisely and make every second count.

Three time truths you must know

Time is the unit of your life and one of your most valuable resources. Therefore, it is imperative you understand the truths about time. These truths will empower you to make the most of your time and your life.

Irrespective of where in the world you are, people are always focussed on time. How long does it take to get from A to B? Do you know how long you will be? What time does the next bus arrive? What time will we meet? How many hours a week do you spend at work? How old are you? All of these questions are asked daily the world over.

Time Truth 1: Even though most people are focussed on time, governed by time and live by the clock, most people have not realised that time management is a myth! It is impossible to manage time. Time runs in a predictable and unchangeable pattern – 60 seconds to a minute, 60 minutes to an hour, 24 hours to a day, 7 days to a week, and so on. No amount of management will ever change the way in which time works. The truth is that you can only manage yourself in the use of time. Time management is actually self management!

Instead of attempting to manage time, you can and should manage yourself in the use of your time. This is the only aspect of your life relating to time that is in your control. This is really good news however, because you have the ability to fully manage yourself in your use of your time. Time management equates to managing your own valuable resources, your energy, your attention and your focus in relation to your available time.

Time Truth 2: All things are not equal to all people. Not everyone is born into equal opportunity; not everyone has equal intelligence, equal height, equal sporting ability, etc. However, the one thing equal to everybody is the number of hours in a day. We all have 24 hours a day. Some people use their 24 hours to achieve amazing results, while others cannot bring themselves to get out of bed. Some people use their 24 hours a day to build multi-million dollar empires, while others achieve very little. Some use their time to contribute to the world around them, imparting their knowledge and skills in a wonderfully significant way, while in contrast, others struggle to manage themselves and realise the gift of each day.

Time Truth 3: Some of the activities you engage in daily are NOT worth your time. As most of your functioning and behaviour is regulated by your subconscious mind, you are not aware of everything you spend your time on. Some of your daily routine is so automatic that you just go through the motions without any real conscious awareness of your actions.

Some of the activities on which you spend your time are not worth your time, while there are other activities you should be incorporating into your daily routine that you are not currently engaging in. Answering the following three questions will assist you to evaluate the activities on which you are spending your time:

1. What are you currently doing that is serving you well?

2. What are you doing that you should STOP doing?

3. What are you not doing that you should START doing?

You are spending your time on your daily activities. Your daily activities are determining the outcomes of your current life.

What you do every day is determining the results of your current life. Your life is habitual. Your daily activities are mostly scheduled and consistent. You use your time – the minutes and hours available daily – for activities, habits and your daily routine. These daily habits produce the outcomes of your life.

POEM

I am your constant companion.
I am your greatest helper or heaviest burden.
I will push you onward or drag you down to failure.
I am completely at your command.
Half of the things you do you might as well turn over
to me and I will do them - quickly and correctly.
I am easily managed - you must be firm with me.
Show me exactly how you want something done and
after a few lessons, I will do it automatically.

I am the servant of great people,
and alas, of all failures as well.
Those who are great, I have made great.
Those who are failures, I have made failures.
I am not a machine though
I work with the precision of a machine
plus the intelligence of a person.
You may run me for profit or run me for ruin -
it makes no difference to me.
Take me, train me, be firm with me, and
I will place the world at your feet.
Be easy with me and I will destroy you.
Who am I? I am Habit.

ANONYMOUS

Are you gaining the optimum advantage from the use of your time?

"Your success is found in your daily routine"
JOHN MAXWELL

Your daily routine or daily habit is delivering the results of your current life. Any result you desire will only ever be achieved by ACTIVITY or action. Taking action is the only way to achieve anything. Activity, over time, produces results, with the results always lagging behind the activity. If you want to get the results you desire in life – a better career, improved loving relationships, a wealthy lifestyle – you need to take action–FIRST.

Author and leadership expert John Maxwell states, "You will never change your life until you change something you do daily." Most of your daily routine is subconsciously driven, habit of that which you have very little awareness. Most of your daily activities are not deliberate and planned actions; they are an attempt to cope with the demands of your environment and life. A reactive and unconsidered daily routine will never produce optimum results. Taking control of your daily routine; thinking proactively, planning and adjusting your daily activities will ensure you spend your 24 hours a day wisely.

What is your ideal routine?

Over time, you have notably created and influenced your current situation. Where you are, whom you are with and what you have is the result of the actions you have or have not taken over time throughout your life. Therefore, your daily routine has, over time, produced your current life.

As mentioned before, your current daily routine is probably a reaction to the demands of your environment. Also, some of your activities are so habitual they are performed automatically, almost like knee-jerk reactions, and you have a very limited conscious awareness of these activities. Famous novelist Agatha Christie said: "Curious things, habits. People themselves never know they have them."

If you leave your current daily routine unchecked and continue to make poor or unsatisfactory decisions regarding your daily activities, the results of your life may be disappointing. Every action you perform holds great power, and this power accumulates over time, resulting in the outcomes of your life. When you choose positive or fulfilling activities, your life will consequently become more positive and fulfilling.

The first step in creating your ideal daily routine is to examine your current daily routine. What activities do you spend your time on? To best observe your current routine, keep a written record of your activities over a two-week period. Write down everything you do in 15-minute intervals. You will be amazed at what you uncover.

Looking at, thinking about and planning a more productive and fulfilling daily, weekly and monthly routine is the next step. Engage in planning your ideal routine like you would an important business trip or vacation abroad. Schedule every activity carefully and mindfully. Using a pen and paper or computer, match the list of activities you are required to do to timeslots across the 24 hour day and 7 day week. A successful routine enables you to take greatest advantage of and balance your four most valuable resources:

✓ Time.

✓ Money.

✓ Focus or attention.

✓ Energy.

Your ideal daily, weekly and monthly routine is a hard copy schedule indicating what you do every 15 minutes. Designing your ideal routine is like solving a brainteaser; it requires careful planning and thought.

Life can be unpredictable and you want to set yourself up to succeed and feel good. Therefore, once you have designed your ideal daily, weekly and monthly routine, the goal is to follow your schedule around 80% of the time, remaining flexible and accommodating when plans change. You never know, one change in your plans could lead to an exciting new venture.

22 Activities you should include in your ideal routine

Below is a list of 22 activities that successful people include in their daily routine. You now have the opportunity to incorporate these activities into your daily routine.

1. Review your extraordinary life folder first thing in the morning.

2. Read from an inspirational book daily.

3. Meditate and pray.

4. Review and visualise your goals.

5. Proclaim your personal power statements – reprogramming your mind for success.

6. Practice visualisation – engaging your imagination.

7. Keep a gratitude journal – write down seven things for which you are grateful, generating feelings of gratitude.

8. Exercise – it sets up your day with health and energy.

9. Eat well and take dietary supplements.

10. Drink your daily water requirement.

11. Review your plan for the day.

12. Engage in your Life's Work.

13. Make effective use of your time – do all you can in one day as effectively as you can in a day.

14. Contact a friend.

15. Engage in personal development through reading and listening to books and other material.

16. Laugh out loud.

17. Learn something new.

18. Review your day.

19. Plan for the next day.

20. Relax.

21. Spend time with people you love.

22. Sleep well.

Your best results will be achieved when you do the following four things:

✓ the right activity – the activity that will produce your desired results.

✓ at the right time – the most opportune timing.

✓ well – the quality of your actions.

✓ consistently over time.

Your life is the direct result of your actions - positive actions lead to a rich life; negative actions lead to a less rewarding life; doing nothing at all will result in achieving nothing.

The Law of Sowing and Reaping controls your activities

In order to reap a harvest, you first must plant a seed. The harvest will always lag behind and be congruent with the seed planted. Just as sowing always comes before reaping, activity always goes before achievement.

Take care when planting your seeds. Ensure you are planting the right seeds - doing the right activities - in order to harvest the life you want. You cannot plant hatred and try to reap a life of love. Nor can you plant manipulation and expect goodness in return.

Sow a thought and reap an emotion; sow an emotion and reap an action; sow an action and reap a routine; sow a routine and reap the outcome of a life.

If you plant good intentions and values in every action with which you engage, you will receive a rich harvest of value and good intentions in return. Remember, you will directly benefit in proportion to the value you add to other people's lives. So, plant your activities mindfully and wisely to ensure you reap generous rewards and results in your future.

Self-discipline is the key to freedom

Doing the right thing at the right time, well, consistently over time will guarantee you achieve the best possible results for your life. For this, self-discipline is a prerequisite! Being disciplined does not mean there will be an army drill sergeant waiting in the sidelines, ensuring you do the right thing at the right time. Self-discipline is the realisation and commitment that you can trust yourself to do what you tell or promise yourself.

Choosing to lead an undisciplined life will prevent you from doing the right thing at the right time. Additionally, making excuses and finding reasons to justify undisciplined actions will ultimately prevent you from achieving the results you desire. Undisciplined actions can create unpleasant consequences and in choosing an undisciplined approach, you hand the control of your life over to your circumstances, creating an undesirable environment and a stressful experience.

Sowing disciplined thought, prioritising, planning and action will reap a life of great reward. Self-discipline leads to tremendous personal freedom!

Your life is a process and a journey...

Your life is a journey, and even though some of the steps you take may seem more exciting than others, each step is of equal importance. Some days will be significant, with many 'ordinary' days in between; but regardless, each and every day you have on earth is equally important. Even though the majority of your journey is comprised of ordinary days, make each day worthwhile and significant. Be present, be mindful and maximise every opportunity and experience. Your life is a journey that requires every step and every day to be complete.

The Ten Laws of Achievement

Applying these ten laws will assist and guide you in living an extraordinary life.

The Ten Laws of Achievement are:

1. Activity = Results. Taking action is essential to achieve anything in life. Without action, there will be no achievement.

2. The results you achieve are directly linked to four things –
   a) What you do - actions you take.
   b) What you don't do - actions not taken.
   c) How you do your actions - the quality of your actions.
   d) When you do them - the timing of your actions.

3. You can get whatever you want if you are prepared to do what it takes to achieve it.

4. You must do whatever is possible and cultivate the optimistic belief that all will turn out well.

5. If you want to achieve different results in life, you must change something you already do. If you continue doing what you have always done, then you will get what you have always got. So, if you don't like the results of you current life, don't try harder to do the same actions you have always done – try something different!

6. Your daily actions taken - your routine - determine your results.

7. Inaction is also an 'action' that will lead to a specific outcome.

8. Doing the most important thing in the most successful manner will bring the best and fastest results.

9. Doing anything is better than doing nothing at all, because you get feedback from any action taken. Even if you make a mistake, it will bring a valuable lesson or growth opportunity.

10. Successful doing involves:
    Thinking ➡ Goal Setting ➡ Planning ➡ Prioritising ➡ Taking Action ➡ Learning from the Feedback ➡ Planning ➡ Prioritising ➡ Taking Action Again.

As William Shakespeare rightly said, "Make use of time, let not advantage slip." Use your time wisely, set your routine thoughtfully, live your life fully. Make each day count.

CHAPTER 13

Engage in Your Life's Work

You are alive for a reason.
Your life is important. You are
on this earth to complete
your Life's Work.

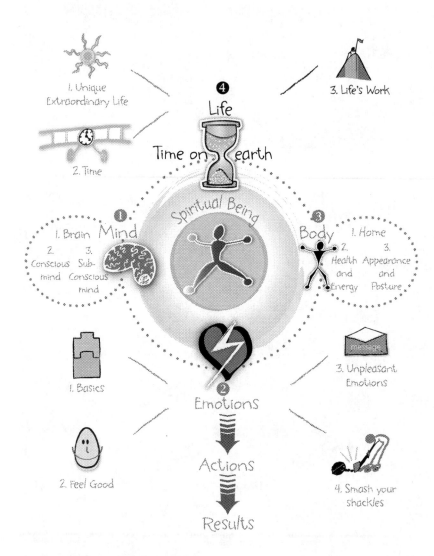

What is your Life's Work?

Your Life's Work is defined as using your unique gifts, talents and ability in your field of interest, to fulfil a need in the world. In short, your Life's Work is: contributing to your environment by doing what you love and what you are good at. A need exists in the world that you were born to fulfil.

Why should you engage in your Life's Work?

Working is a given part of our way of life. You can correctly assume you will engage in some form of work throughout most of your life. Even if you choose to be a stay-at-home parent, it is a vocation, not a vacation. Therefore, if working is a given, wouldn't life be much more enjoyable if you could work to your strengths, be good at what you do and enjoy your work?

Performing your Life's Work guarantees you will:

- ✓ Work to your strengths.

- ✓ Be good at what you do.

- ✓ Be passionate about your work.

- ✓ Enjoy what you do.

- ✓ As a bonus, contribute to the world in a significant and meaningful manner.

- ✓ Be fulfilling a world need by doing what you love.

If you are going to work anyway, why would you choose to be 'stuck' doing something other than your Life's Work? Doing your Life's Work is very gratifying and rewarding and it satisfies a need in the world. A true win-win situation.

The world is filled with need

Watching and listening to the news gives you a sense of the need that exists in the world. The world seems to be a needy place, offering ample opportunity for you to contribute and assist. The good news, therefore, is that this need creates an opportunity for you to do what you love and what you are good at. Doing your Life's Work will not be burdensome; it is contributing to your world by doing what you love and are good at.

For example, a need exists in the world for people to eat and enjoy food. This need creates an opportunity for some people to become chefs and cooks. If you are gifted and talented at cooking and passionate about food, then being a chef or cook might be your Life's Work. If so, your body will have the capability to fully experience the subtle flavours and textures of any food you taste.

You will also take great pleasure in creating wonderful eating experiences for others. In short, you will be good at cooking, love feeding people and be passionate about food. Your Life's Work will be to create wonderful eating experiences for others, thus contributing to your environment by doing what you love and what you are good at.

Seasons of your Life's Work...

As with your life, your Life's Work moves through seasons or phases. Each phase in your quest to discover, define and engage in your Life's Work will follow a path through a season. Just like the natural seasons that exist in the world, there is a progression from one phase to another. There are four seasons relating to your Life's Work:

1. Preparation phase.
2. Seeking phase.
3. Defining phase.
4. Engaging phase.

Preparation Phase:

This is the first phase of your Life's Work journey. During your preparation phase, you grow, develop and prepare for your Life's Work. Your preparation began from the moment you were born and continues through your childhood and into your young adult life. This phase of your life may take as little as five years or sixty-five years to complete.

Seeking Phase:

Your second phase is heralded when you become aware there is something more to your life than what you are currently experiencing. You sense there is something missing in your life; something more you wish to accomplish; a need to decide on your occupation, or an awareness you need to view what you are doing in a different way. It is a time where you develop a sense that you are not engaged in the work that will ultimately satisfy and energise you. This encourages you to seek out your Life's Work. The age at which you will progress though this phase is unique to you, but you will recognise your seeking phase by a sense of restlessness and seeking; a sense that you must define that which you were born to do.

This is a restless phase with questions and quests driving you to find your Life's Work. It is marked with dissatisfaction concerning your current situation. The seeking phase is your quest for uncovering the work for which you were ultimately created. Sadly, many people never progress beyond this phase, as they tend to look for the answer in all the wrong places. If you are stuck in the seeking phase, become excited! At the end of this chapter there is information on how to uncover your Life's Work.

This becomes a time when you want to define what it is that you should be doing in order to live a life filled with greater satisfaction, enjoyment and significance. It allows you to take control of where you want your life to head, seek out the unique gifts you possess and determine how you can contribute effectively to the world. This is an important phase in your life – you are seeking your Life's Work.

Defining Phase:

Your defining phase is your opportunity to define and write a Life's Work statement - a broad understanding of your Life's Work and the direction in which you will be heading. This is the foundation to defining the specifics of what your Life's Work will entail, allowing you to take the steps towards engaging with your Life's Work.

Engaging and Doing Phase:

This is the most exciting and rewarding phase of the process; it is where you actively engage with your Life's Work. You are now able to commence with or work towards your Life's Work, contributing to your environment by doing what you are good at and what you love to do.

Initially, you will have to earn the right to do your Life's Work by training and developing the required skills and knowledge. This will also require you to make an investment or down payment into your Life's Work; something you will probably have to do before others will believe in your Life's Work.

You will now be able to move into the stage of contributing to the world; granting the world the benefit of your strengths, passion, energy and attention. It is also a time where you are able to see a return on your investment, as you too benefit from doing your Life's Work.

Once you have progressed through each season, you will engage in all four stages simultaneously. As you travel on your journey, you will grow in experience and knowledge, inadvertently preparing and being prepared for your future Life's Work. You will also seek, think and dream about your future - what your next Life's Work contribution will be. Your Life's Work statement is a broad understanding of your Life's Work, pointing to a direction. However, as you grow and progress on your journey, your understanding of the specifics of what you are meant to do will grow and develop too. You will constantly define and redefine your Life's Work and the opportunities to contribute to your world in a more meaningful way.

To fully complete your Life's Work, you will be required to reach your full potential. You will find yourself growing and stretching in attempt to fulfil your Life's Work, however each stage through which you move allows you to gain greater access to your full potential as you prepare for, seek, define and engage in your Life's Work.

You are uniquely designed for your Life's Work

All your strengths, talents and interests align with your Life's Work. Have you noticed that other people are not quite like you? Have you noticed that people are different? Every person is uniquely designed for his or her Life's Work.

Simplistic examples offer further explanation:
Tom is blessed with a natural attention to detail. He wants things to be 'right' and enjoys analysing and working with a lot of information. Tom also prefers to work alone. He has always been interested in figures and finances and is energised by accuracy. As a result, Tom is uniquely designed to be an accountant.

Peter has always wanted to help people. Being alone does not make Peter feel good and he prefers an environment that offers a lot of people interaction. Peter is caring in nature and has always been interested in the body and how it functions. He is a natural team player and finds meaning in helping others. Peter is uniquely designed to be a nurse.

There are people uniquely designed for every need that exists in the world. There are astronauts, stay-at-home parents, doctors, teachers, supermarket workers, business owners, pool cleaners, gardeners, TV presenters, authors, entrepreneurs, undertakers, florists, photographers, volunteer workers, carers and thousands of other vocations. Your Life's Work is your vocation, your passion, your strengths and your unique contribution to the world. It is contributing to your environment by doing what you love.

Take the lead

It is quite possible that no one will congratulate you or sing your praises when you discover and engage with your Life's Work. Additionally, no one will give you permission or create an opportunity for you to do your Life's Work. In all probability, others could very well disapprove of your 'new found direction' and the change you will be making in your life.

It is quite possible those around you will try to persuade you to stay in your current role as homemaker, CEO, sales person, etc., giving as many excuses as they can think of to hold you back. At this point in your journey you must take the lead, back yourself and your dreams, and overcome your own doubt and opposition from your environment. Without fear, there is no courage; and without opposition, there is no victory.

As you engage in your Life's Work, reveal to those around you the contribution you are making and the joy you are finding as you improve your world by doing what you love. Once they see just how much you are gaining from your contribution, they will begin to change their attitude and approve of your decision. Inspired by your courage, contribution and the resulting success and joy you have achieved, these people will then want to join in and be part of what you are creating. But first you must believe in yourself, your Life's Work and take the lead role.

You must earn the right

It is quite possible you will have to earn the right to do your Life's Work. A doctor has to study, train and sacrifice many valuable aspects of their life to 'earn the right' to contribute to the world as a doctor. In the same way, you will have to earn the right to do your Life's Work.

It is sowing the seeds before you can harvest a crop. You may have to train, study, volunteer, work free of charge, develop infrastructure, invest in help from others and give of yourself and your resources to your Life's Work before you reap the reward. Back yourself, believe in your Life's Work and invest confidently and astutely in it!

When will my Life's Work be completed?

For as long as you exist and live in your human form, you have your Life's Work to do. Your Life's Work will be completed the day your human life ends. If you have engaged in your Life's Work, then this day marks its completion. However, if you failed to define and engage in your Life's Work, the day of your death marks the end of your opportunity to do so. Remember though, your Life's Work will change as you grow and mature. Likewise your understanding of what your Life's Work is will change and develop as you progress through the different stages of your life. Irrespective of your age, as long as you are alive, you are yet to complete your Life's Work.

What will your return on investment be?

By giving of yourself, your time and your talents to the world, you will gain more life, meaning and significance in return.

The six major personal benefits from doing your Life's Work are:

1. Ultimately gaining joy and fulfilment by doing what you love.

2. Completing your Life's Work adds meaning to your life.

3. Embarking on a journey that allows you to grow and develop to be all you can be, creating the opportunity for you to reach your full potential.

4. A clarity, focus, passion and aim; it gives you a purpose or a reason to exist.

5. Drawing your attention away from the trivial issues in day-to-day life, allowing you to focus on what is truly important – to apply yourself and your life in a meaningful manner.

6. Receiving material abundance and financial reward to the degree to which you create and demonstrate value for others.

You are not the only beneficiary when you complete your Life's Work; the world around you also benefits greatly from your contributions. Engaging in your Life's Work is in no way about being selfish; rather it is about selflessness, contribution and serving the human world in your own unique way.

Can your Life's Work be insignificant?

The answer to this is NO! Every person's Life's Work is important, significant and meaningful. Whether your Life's Work is to assist people in paying for their groceries, to be the CEO of a large company, a stay-at-home mum, an artist, a teacher or any other conceivable endeavour, your work is important and significant. There is a person for every job, for every need and for every opportunity. So, embrace your Life's Work; it is important and meaningful.

How much of your Life's Work will you understand at any point in time?

At no stage of your life will you be able to see the full extent of your Life's Work. You might have a full understanding of the direction you will take in doing your Life's Work, but not of every step of the way. Your understanding of how to contribute by doing your Life's Work will grow as you grow and you should remain flexible and open to opportunities to contribute. However, be careful to recognise distractions and take care not to veer away from the direction of your Life's Work.

As you travel on your journey discovering your Life's Work, opportunities will open up, showing you alternative paths. These paths may take you to areas previously discounted, or you may not have even realised existed, and these paths could bring you even greater fulfilment than before.

What happens if you begin to doubt your life's work?

Doubt and fear are often common elements in the process. However, as stated in chapter 6, you can feel the fear and do it anyway. Doubt is also a natural part of moving into a new direction or new venture. Be courageous and push through the doubt and fear; crossing the bridge into a significant life of contribution.

When you are engaged in your Life's Work and you continue to experience doubt, it is a sign you need to check your motives and motivation. Has your focus shifted from your original purpose, away from your contribution of using your time on earth to fulfil a need within the world?

What happens if you do not complete your life's work?

Even though as humans we share many similarities, each person is unique. You are unique. A void exists in the world that only you can fill and there are needs only you can satisfy. Only you are able to complete your Life's Work. Your Life's Work is unique to you and if you fail to discover and engage in it, sadly it will remain undone.

The vast need that exists in the world is an indication of the number of people failing to do their life's work. No one else can complete the work you were created to do and no one else can contribute to the world in the exact same manner as you.

What if you are already engaged in your Life's Work?

If you are fortunate enough to be engaged in your Life's Work already, you will still benefit from writing a Life's Work statement. This process will engage your conscious mind to increase your awareness and mindfulness of your Life's Work. Greater awareness will enable you to pick up on more opportunities in your environment for greater contribution and success in completing your Life's Work.

How do you discover your Life's Work?

You possess many talents, gifts, strengths and abilities. The responsibility falls to you to discover, develop and contribute your talents, gifts, strengths and abilities to those around you.

The clues to your Life's Work are found in you.

For a detailed step-by-step process you can follow to discover your Life's Work, please go www.nakedtruthaboutyou.com.

Even if you are already engaged in your Life's Work, a Life's Work Statement can be very helpful, go to www.nakedtruthaboutyou.com/statement for instructions and examples.

As soon as you have defined what your Life's Work entails, take full responsibility for its completion. Remember, if you do not engage with your Life's Work and meet that specific need that exists in the world, your work will sadly remain undone. Only you have the ability to fulfil your Life's Work.

CHAPTER 14

Face the Big Four: Change, Problems, Goals and Others' Opinions of You!

Life is predictably unpredictable

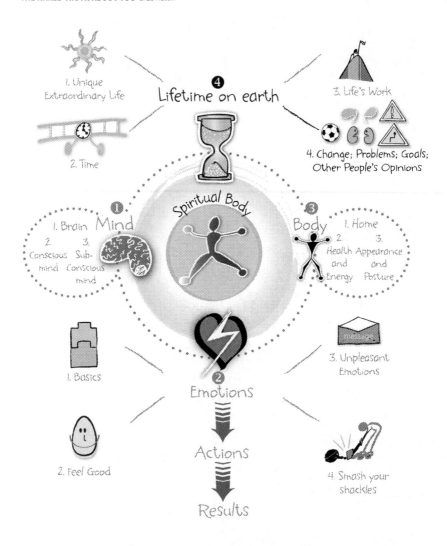

A young man sits patiently on a park bench, waiting for the next bus. On his lap, he holds a box of chocolates. After a few moments, the young man turns to the lady next to him, removes the lid of the box and asks if she would like a chocolate. The lady accepts graciously and he returns the lid to the chocolate box.

Gazing down at the box he says, "Like my Momma always says, life is like a box of chocolates. You never know what you're gonna get."

The scene is from the highly acclaimed 1994 film 'Forrest Gump', starring Tom Hanks. As illustrated in this scene, life is predictably unpredictable. You just don't know what will come your way. However, it is safe to assume you will face obstacles, challenges and situations at some point in your life. Change, problems, goals and other people's opinion of you are given elements of life. This chapter has been created to show you how to use these obstacles to your advantage and ensure you benefit from them.

While you are resisting change, you are changing anyway.

Think of yourself as a tree; you are either constantly growing or slowly dying – there is no 'staying the same' position. This is a fact of life – you are growing, maturing and developing, or slowly weakening, deteriorating and dying. Change is automatic and inevitable. The control you have in your life is to determine whether you will grow in maturity and strength, or allow yourself to weaken and deteriorate.

At birth, you were undeveloped and immature. Then, as you physically grew and developed through childhood and your young adult life, you also grew in maturity. Even though the development and growth of your body ceases in young adulthood, the development and growth of your character and who you are as a person should be an ongoing process. One of the reasons for your life on earth is to develop and grow from immaturity to maturity, reaching your full potential throughout your time on earth.

The reward for living life is...

It is not what you possess or what you achieve with your time on earth that produces lasting rewards, but who you become through the process. The personal development, maturity, improvement and growth you experience become the lasting rewards to living life well. After all, your earthly possessions and achievements hold limited worth. You will leave this world just the same as you entered it - with no earthly possessions. The eventual aim of your existence, therefore, is to become all you can be as a Spiritual Being through becoming all you can be as a human being.

What does it mean to grow?

Going from immature to mature involves growth. Can you grow and stay the same? The answer is obviously NO! All growth and development involves change. Growth invokes positive change.

But you hate change!

As discussed in chapter 6 on emotions, people resist change for fear of experiencing the unpleasant 'change emotions'. Due to this resistance to change, you require other influences to create opportunities for you to change, to persuade you to change, to coerce you to change, to push you to change or even to force you into positive change and growth when necessary.

Life offers three change catalysts

Because of people's natural resistance to change, life presents you with three catalysts for change. These three catalysts create growth opportunities and assist you to change.

The three change and growth opportunities are:

1. Problems.

2. Goals.

3. Other people's opinion of you.

Growth Opportunity 1: Problems

Problems are an indication of life. While you are alive, you will face problems. Everybody faces problems throughout their lives. This is fortunate for two reasons: firstly, for as long as you are facing problems, you are still alive; and secondly, problems create the opportunity for you to develop, grow and mature.

Problems insist that you change. They say to you, 'It is time for personal development; it is time for you to grow and change'. Problems can be your friend - they can help and assist you, even force you into personal development and growth, insisting you change.

While problems create growth opportunities and insist that you change, you determine the effects of your problems on you and your life; you determine the outcomes and end result. Your ability and attitude will determine whether you grow, or whether the problem results in your demise. Therefore, your ability and willingness to grow from these situations and the determination to take on the changes needed, will ultimately decide whether you overcome your problems, or allow them to overcome you. Problems guarantee change, but you determine whether the change will be constructive or destructive.

Seven keys to solving any problem

These keys can be applied to any problem you might face. Applying these principles will ensure you gain benefit from your problems.

1. Problems are an indication of life.

When faced with a problem, feel encouraged – you are still alive. Problems indicate life. Problems are a sign of life. While you do not have a choice in facing problems, you do choose the results and effects of the problems you face.

2. **The problems you face are designed to grow you.**

   Every problem you face is specifically designed for your personal development. Your problems are custom-made for you. Your ability and willingness to grow and change will determine whether you overcome your
   problem or your problem overcomes you. You ultimately control the effect your problems will have on you and your life, and if you take advantage of the opportunities your problems create, they will be your friends;
   assisting you in your journey of personal growth and development.
   You may be currently experiencing a problem that feels insurmountable
   and cumbersome, but remember, this problem is designed for you to
   overcome and grow in the process.

3. **There are two types of problems: Problems of success and problems
   of failure.**

   The grade or quality of the problem you are likely to experience is determined by your own personal development. For example, universally experienced problems are money problems. Rich, middle class and poor alike
   face money problems; however the quality of the money problems they
   face is significantly different. The rich consider things such as a volatile
   stock market, diminished returns on investment portfolios and lower than
   expected dividends, as being a problem (problem of success). Whereas the
   poor might struggle to find enough money to put food on the table for
   their family and worry about paying the utility bills (problem of lesser quality). As you grow and develop in ability and character through overcoming
   your problems, so will the quality of the problems you face improve.

4. **Never look for someone else to blame, rather use the same energy to
   'fix it!'**

   The old adage of 'If life hands you lemons, make lemonade' holds true.
   The energy used in searching for someone to blame is wasted energy.
   When you know who to blame, you are still no closer to a solution than
   before.

   Listen to your problems; they are speaking to you. At first it is a whisper
   saying, 'This is a problem you should sort out'. When a problem speaks to
   you, it is your responsibility to lean in and overcome the problem; this is
   your opportunity to grow. If you do not listen to the whisper, the problem grows in magnitude and will begin to raise its voice to get your at-

tention. This may feel as though you have been hit over the head with a baseball bat. If you remain in blame mode, waiting for someone else to sort out your problem, it will develop and gain more momentum. At this point, your problem will start to scream at you, possibly resulting in you feeling like you have been hit by a bus. Consequently, heeding the whispers is a much more pleasant way of dealing with your problems.

Choose to apply your limited time and energy successfully; heed the message and find a solution to the problem, learning the lessons and developing in the process.

5. **Lean into your problems, engage with them, push back at them and wrestle them to the ground.**
    Never try to run away or avoid your problems; they will grow in magnitude, be harder to solve and might overcome you. Lean into the problem, understand what it is about and engage with it. This will enable you to wrestle it to the ground - to dominate it before it dominates you. Never try to run away from the problem, it will always follow you; it will grow and manifest into something much bigger and harder to solve. Face your problems head on and push back at them, and you will overcome!

6. **Be careful to solve the right problem.**
    Don't treat the symptom, treat the cause. Always ask the questions: 'Am I solving the real problem? Am I addressing the heart of the issue?'

Take care to solve your real problems, don't just place a band-aid over the symptom; treat the cause. Think of it as a skin rash that appears at the most inopportune time. You consult your doctor, expecting and wanting an ointment to quickly fix the problem. However, your doctor identifies more than just a rash and orders blood tests to determine the cause of the rash. The results indicate you are allergic to the chemicals in your washing powder. Hence, the doctor has found out the cause of your rash and gives you the right treatment for your problem.

In the same way, it is important to ponder your problems and establish the real cause. Consider the problem you are experiencing; are you engaging with the heart of the problem or are you being distracted by the symptoms?

7.   **Never call a problem a problem.**

As discussed in chapters 3, 4 and 5, your mind is a powerful tool. Most people have bad programs running in their subconscious mind regarding problems. The word 'problem' will often evoke feelings of fear, doubt and hopelessness, and a feeling of being overwhelmed.

Make solving your problems as easy as possible by never referring to a problem as a problem; refer to them as growth opportunities, challenges or even situations. This allows your mind the freedom to overcome your challenges instead of being bogged down in your problems.

Note: For ease of discussion, the term problem will be used throughout this chapter.

Seven keys to being an effective solution finder

Finding solutions is the way to overcome your challenges (problems). Your ability to find solutions to your challenges will determine how quickly and easily you learn, grow and move on. Finding the right solution for the right challenge will enable you to grow and learn more quickly and easily, improving your ability, character and life in the process.

1.   **The solution is contained within problem.**

Engaging with the problem will reveal the solution - the solution for every problem is hidden within the problem. Avoiding the problem will result in never finding the solution.

Remember to clearly define the outcome you want to achieve in resolving the problem. Answering the following question will assist you in defining this outcome: "What will my situation be / look like / feel like when I have resolved this problem?'

Wrestling with your problem will expose the solution.

2.   **Be creative.**

The more possible alternative approaches or possible solutions you have for your problem, the more likely you will reach your goal and overcome your problem. Creativity is key to finding alternative approaches and better ways to resolve your problems. Be creative in finding more than one way to achieve the same goal.

Practical ways of stimulating your creativity:

The aim is to get your mind into alpha waves to unleash your creativity. This can be achieved by:

  ✓ Listening to classical music.

  ✓ Spending time walking in nature.

  ✓ Watching the waves of the ocean.

  ✓ Discussing possible solutions with a friend while walking.

  ✓ Keeping a pen and paper next to your bed to write down the thoughts that come to you as you are falling asleep or waking up in the morning.

  ✓ Sitting completely still for 30 minutes.

3. **Be flexible.**

   Trying harder to do the same thing, expecting a different result, is what many define as insanity. Once you have defined different approaches to solving your problem, be flexible in moving from one approach to another. Don't get caught trying harder to do something when you should be trying something entirely different. Allow yourself to act on the new and innovative ideas you will generate through the use of your creativity.

4. **Be resourceful.**

   Every problem you face is designed as an opportunity for you to grow and develop. Therefore, you will never face a problem that you do not have the resources to overcome. Open your eyes to what you have at hand right now. You either possess or have access to every resource you will require to take the next step in overcoming your problems. You might have to be creative in the way you apply your resources though. A spoon might become a shovel, and a pen might become a stirring device.

5. Be active.

Less talking and more doing! Take action and keep working towards find-ing a solution. Even if you only inch forward, every inch takes you closer to overcoming your problems. Complaining, worrying and blaming others does not achieve anything. Activity = results. Be active and take consid-ered action!

6. Keep learning from your actions, receive the feedback and change your approach.

As you take considered action, you will achieve a result. It is important to accept the feedback that this result offers. Some of your actions might not produce the intended results. Some of your actions might even cause you to feel you are failing. However, remember that failure is only failure if you fail to learn the lesson. Trying an approach and failing is not fail-ing at all; it is taking you one step closer to successfully overcoming your problems. Failure and mistakes teach you what not to do.

Be on the lookout for feedback from the results of your actions, learn from it, adjust your behaviour and try again. Soon your problem will be solved.

7. Here's to baby steps, doing what you can with what you have!

Whatever your problem might be, keep your desired outcomes in sight. Remind yourself this is a learning opportunity and the lessons you learn will be invaluable. By controlling your mind, body and emotions during this time, you will control the challenge. Remember, any step in the right direction is a good step, no matter how small. Baby steps are the founda-tion to walking tall!

Growth Opportunity 2: Goals

When you set a goal you create your own opportu-nity for personal development and growth. In the pursuit of your goals you will stretch, grow, improve, mature and develop.

Goal setting is the process of defining what you desire, an essential skill for doing your Life's Work, for personal development and for living an extraordinary life. Many people struggle with setting goals as they do not know what they want. An easy way to overcome this pitfall is to answer the question' What don't you want?' first. This will allow you to gain insight into what you do want. Goal setting is the process of writing down what you want.

Seven golden rules for easy goal setting

1. **Goals give direction.**

   The ideal way to set a goal is to focus on what you desire. When you focus on something, you will ultimately possess it. However, if you focus on nothing specific, you will achieve nothing specific. When there is nothing to drive you forward, to strive for or to give you direction, you will achieve very little. The same principle applies to when you focus on what you don't want. Vocalising and dwelling upon the things you don't want in your life will present you with the very things you despise.

2. **Goals focus your mind, allowing you to see opportunity.**

   You go where you look. Any motorbike rider will tell you not to focus on the tree, as you are sure to ride straight into it. Focussing on your goals will allow you to achieve your goals over time. As discussed in chapter 4, the function of your conscious mind, perception, allows you to see what you are focussed on. Focussing on your goals will enable your mind to see the opportunities that you will require to achieve your goals.

3. **Goals create growth opportunities.**

   Setting goals gives you something outside your reach to work towards. This creates the opportunity for you to grow and develop as you stretch to achieve your goals.

4. **Any goal is better than no goal.**

   Many people feel they need to set "perfect" goals or the "right" type of goals. However, this mindset prevents them from ever setting a goal. In the end, there is no such thing as the perfect or right goal; initially, any goal is better than no goal at all.

   Setting goals does not prohibit or prevent you from achieving another goal – your life is a process, a journey if you will, but it is important to be flexible, as new goals will present themselves as you grow. It is also necessary to set deadlines for your goals, because without deadlines, your goals will seem to become unobtainable and will be pushed further out of your mind, resulting in you never achieving what you want. As you work through and achieve your goals (and they do need to be worked on), set yourself new and more challenging goals for the future.

5. **Set positive and smart goals.**

Ensure the goals you set are SMART. This means your goals are:

Specific
Measureable
Achievable
Result orientated
Timeframe/deadline

Define your goals using positive language, always stating what you want. For example, if you set a goal such as - "I don't want to be lonely when I am old" – you are setting an unproductive goal. In fact, it is a poor choice for a goal, as your mind will focus on the negative of 'being lonely' and you will undoubtedly experience loneliness in your future. However, if you reword the goal as – "I want to be surrounded by people when I am old" – the positivity ensures you will get what you want.

6. **Set be goals, do goals and achieve goals.**

Broaden your goals by setting goals for who you want to be or your character, what you want to do with and during your lifetime, as well as what you want to achieve or have in your life.

✓ 'Be goals' – are goals for who you want to become. They are personal development goals.

✓ 'Do goals' – are goals of what you want to do during your life.

✓ 'Achieve goals' – are goals of things you would like to achieve, have and own.

7. Write your goals down.

Keep a written record of the goals you set, reviewing your goals daily. In setting goals, the aim is to ensure they have CLARITY. Clarity x Action = Achievement

Use your imagination when setting your goals – you can achieve, be and do anything you want in your mind. Your imagination is a veritable playground of possibilities. When using your imagination to set goals, check your emotional response to the types of goals you set. Do these goals make you excited and nervous simultaneously? If so, these are the right goals for you.

Growth Opportunity 3: Other people's opinions of you

Have you ever been told you shouldn't care what other people think of you? It is almost certain you have. It is highly likely that you are often confronted with other people's opinions of you. It is also highly likely that you care about what they might think of you, even though everybody tells you that you shouldn't.

You were trained to be concerned about other people's opinions of you. In early life, you were trained to believe your parents' opinions are very important. As you entered the schooling system, you were taught your teachers would evaluate not only you as a person, but also your work, and that the teachers' opinions were very important indeed. As a teenager, your peer group's opinions carried great weight. Ironically, after all of that training and programming, one of the first things you are told as an adult is: you shouldn't care what other people think of you.

In reality, society functions because most people are concerned with what others think of them. Your concern about other's opinions of you keeps your behaviour in check. Observing society's rules becomes more important in the light of other's opinions regarding your behaviour.

You are probably concerned with other people's opinions, and so you should be! This creates another valuable growth opportunity for you. Living up to the expectations of others provides us with the incentive to lift our game, try harder, do more and be better.

Seven keys to making others' opinions of you count

1. **Care about what other people think of you.**
    Being honest with yourself and accepting that you are concerned about others' opinions of you creates an opportunity for personal development and growth.

2. **Define what you want others to think about you.**
    Define consciously and mindfully what you would like other people to think about you. Do you want to be known as caring, smart, successful or loving? Defining the person you would like others to see when they observe you creates the opportunity to be and become that person. Define who you would like to BE, what you would like to DO and what you would like to ACHIEVE in your life.

3. **Program your subconscious mind for easy success.**
    Take the list you created from the above exercise and turn it into personal power statements. Using the suggestions in chapter 5, program your subconscious mind to be, do and achieve the newly defined you. Here is a reminder how to reporgram your subconscious mind.

The secret to reprogramming your subconscious mind

Reprogramming your mind is surprisingly easy! It is a three-step process you can employ immediately to program your mind for success. Success is defined as: being the powerful YOU and living an extraordinary life.

Start to program and reprogram your mind for success now!

Step 1: Define the good programs that will allow you to be your best and live extraordinarily. Create a list of all of the attributes you want to have and all the programs and the beliefs that will ensure success.

Step 2: Input these new programs into your subconscious mind via your conscious mind by repeatedly saying, listening to, writing and visualising these new programs.

Step 3: Incorporate this process into your daily routine and be disciplined at reprogramming your subconscious mind.

4. **Set goals that will create the life you want others to see.**
   Referring to what you want to do and achieve in your life, set SMART and positive goals. Review your goals daily.

5. **Work out an action plan to ensure you achieve your goals.**
   Write down the answer to the question, 'What do I need to do to achieve my first goal?' Then, answer the following question, 'By when will I take the action?' and schedule the activity accordingly. Now to the next questions, 'What do I need to do to achieve this goal? By when?' Repeat this process until you have made an action plan for all of your goals. An action plan is a list of activities, scheduled by when the activity will be done.

6. **Start acting and working consciously and diligently.**
   Stick to your action plan, taking action when scheduled as required.

7. **Be the person, do the things and enjoy the life that you defined.**
   Just be, do and achieve all that you want to!

A simple seven-step process to overcome problems, achieve goals and get the most out of other people's opinions of you

Here is a universal process you can use to overcome your problems, achieve your goals and be the person you want to be. This process is simple – you only need a pen or pencil, a piece of blank paper and your diary, to create your plan to succeed.

When you start this process, ensure you find a nice quiet place in which to work through your plan, allowing your mind to clear. After you finish your plan, place a copy of your goals in your extraordinary life folder as well as somewhere you will most likely look each day, such as your bathroom mirror or near your computer. This way each day you can affirm the goals you wish to achieve for your life.

Step 1: State the goal or your ideal clearly.

- ✓ Always use positive language and write down in as much detail as possible the ideal situation you would like to achieve.

- ✓ If you are dealing with a problem, the goal is the situation you want to achieve after you have resolved or overcome the problem - the ideal situation you want to be in after the challenge.

- ✓ Write down your goal clearly and specifically.

- ✓ Be optimistic about your future and your goals or ideals. Never believe that your goals are unobtainable – everything is within your grasp, you just need to go for it!

Step 2: State your current situation.

- ✓ Write down in as much detail as possible what your current situation is.

- ✓ The best map in the world will not get you to Sydney if you do not know where you are. If you do not know what your starting point is, you will never know how to get to where you want to be.

- ✓ Be brutally honest about your current situation, because if you are not honest, you will only be cheating yourself.

Step 3: Make a plan to build a bridge from where you are to where you want to go.

- ✓ Brainstorm a list of activities and actions to get you from where you are to where you want to be - use your imagination!

- ✓ Prioritise your list.

- ✓ Schedule the activities.

Step 4: Commence moving in the direction of your goal / ideal.

- ✓ Baby steps forward are better than a slow deterioration of your situation.

- ✓ Commence immediately with the most important action / activity to get your journey started.

✓ Do the doing.

Step 5: Program your subconscious mind for easy achievement.

✓ Turn your goals and activities into personal power statements and program your subconscious mind for easy achievement.

Step 6: Keep reviewing and working on your plan until you have reached your goal or ideal.

✓ As you move in the direction of your goal or ideal, not everything you try will work.

✓ Learn from your feedback, mistakes and perceived failures. Adjust your plan and keep moving in the direction of your goals and ideals.

Step 7: Reach your goal or ideal and celebrate!

The ultimate reward in life is not what you achieve, but who you become! You have many daily opportunities for personal growth and development. Take advantage of your problems, goals and other people's opinions of you and ensure you gain maximum benefit from them.

CHAPTER 15

Accept You Are a Spiritual Being

Within your body is a Spiritual Being. Within your body is YOU!

YOU are a spiritual being having a human experience!

Within your body is a Spiritual Being. Within your body is YOU! This Spiritual Being is the mirror image of your human being, yet it exists as spirit or energy, and not human matter. YOU, in spirit, are identical to you in physical form, yet the substance in which YOU exist is different. You consist of two identical reflections or versions; one physical and the other spiritual, both melded together to form who you are today.

YOU are an immortal spiritual being

YOU, in spirit, are immortal and eternal. While your human body, mind and emotions act as the vehicle for YOU in this life, YOU will continue to exist long after your human mind, body and emotions have passed away. When your life comes to an end and your human body, mind and emotions die, YOU, as a Spiritual Being, will be liberated from your human experience and continue to exist as a Spiritual Being in your spiritual form. Your human form is temporary, while YOU in spiritual form will exist forever. YOU, in spirit, are superior to you in body, mind and emotions!

Who is in control?

Who is controlling your life - your human vehicle or YOU? Are YOU allowing your human tools and vehicle to control your actions, behaviour and life? As long as your human form is in control, your life will not be all it can be. Therefore, allowing your human primal mind, body and emotions to control YOU, will never achieve the extraordinary life for which you are destined!

Consider for a moment whether your mind, body, or emotions are controlling any aspect of your life. Remember, YOU have the power to take charge over your life once again - there is no justifiable reason for your human mind, emotions, or body to control YOU and hinder YOU from living extraordinarily!

Body:

YOU are not your body. Does your human body tell YOU to overeat or consume too much junk food, alcohol or drugs? Do YOU obey it? Your human body exists with many primal lusts, wants and needs. Do these human lusts, wants and needs control your life? Or do YOU, as a Spiritual Being, control your human body and benefit from its use? Do YOU care for your body, keeping it in check and keeping it strong, so YOU can use it to greatest benefit?

Mind:

YOU are not your thoughts. YOU are a Spiritual Being who has been given a mind as a tool to enable YOU to live an extraordinary life. Do YOU control your mind, your thinking and your programming? Are YOU taking responsibility for using your mind to enable you to live your life to the full and fulfil your Life's Work by contributing to and improving your world by doing what you love?

Emotions:

YOU are not your feelings. YOU are a Spiritual Being having a human experience through your emotions. By mastering and controlling your emotions, you control the actions you take and the outcomes you achieve as a result. As you master and control your emotions, YOU powerfully influence your life experience and quality of life. By generating productive emotions and feelings, YOU will be able to do your best work and live an extraordinary life.

It's up to YOU

YOU set the tone for how people respond to you. If YOU love yourself, others will love you too! If YOU believe in yourself, others will believe in you too! If YOU feel you are attractive, others will find you attractive too. If YOU respect yourself, you will be treated with respect in return! If YOU trust yourself to keep the promises you make to YOURSELF, others will trust you too. If YOU admire and appreciate your mind, body and emotions, others will do the same in return. Whatever YOU require to live an extraordinary life is within your grasp. It is up to YOU – YOU set the tone for how others will perceive and respond to you!

Spirit relates to spirit

Spirit relates to Spirit, and spirit can only be satisfied by Spirit. So how can YOU be satisfied? How can YOU ensure YOUR spiritual needs and desires are fulfilled?

God is the ultimate Spirit! The only way to truly satisfy YOUR spirit is by entering into a loving and reverent relationship with Him. YOU are a creation of God and He longs for a relationship with YOU. God also placed in YOUR spirit a yearning for a relationship with Him. Many people misinterpret this yearning and subsequently try to fulfil the spiritual yearning with physical things. However, there is nothing in the physical world that will ever satisfy YOUR spirit. Trying to satisfy YOUR spiritual desires with earthly things is futile and a waste of your precious time on earth. YOUR spirit cannot be satisfied by body, mind or emotions. YOUR spirit can only ever be satisfied by the ultimate Spirit, God!

God has YOUR best interest at heart and desires that YOU become, do and have all you can in this life and the next. God is waiting for YOU to reach out to Him, to seek a relationship with Him. YOU will live the extraordinary life for which you are destined when YOU seek God and foster a loving relationship with Him over time.

Why are YOU living this human experience?

YOU have been granted this opportunity to live as a human being for a very specific reason; a reason of eternal significance!

The reason for YOUR human experience here on earth is to develop and prepare YOUR inner spiritual being for YOUR eternal existence. Your time here on earth, in human form, is an opportunity for YOU, the Spiritual Being, to learn, prepare, develop and mature. As YOUR spiritual form is a mirror image or reflection of your human form, the growth and development of your spiritual form is interrelated to the growth and development of your human form. YOU grow and mature through the process of mastering your mind, body and emotions and creating an extraordinary life. This is achieved through personal growth and development, allowing your Spiritual Being to grow and develop alongside your human form.

To ensure you live extraordinarily, YOU must:

✓ Enter into and maintain an intimate and loving relationship with God.

✓ Love yourself.

✓ Master your mind, body and emotions.

✓ Strive to do your best.

✓ Use your human tools, gifts and talents to make the world a better place.

✓ Pursue what you want and need through serving other people.

✓ Contribute to other people in your own unique way.

✓ Love the people around you.

✓ Always act ethically and honestly.

✓ Consider the needs of other people.

✓ Strive to be a loving, compassionate and forgiving person.

As you grow in strength and maturity as a human being, YOU will grow in strength and maturity as a Spiritual Being! This growth and preparation will ensure you not only live an extraordinary human experience, but that YOU also have an extraordinary eternal experience!

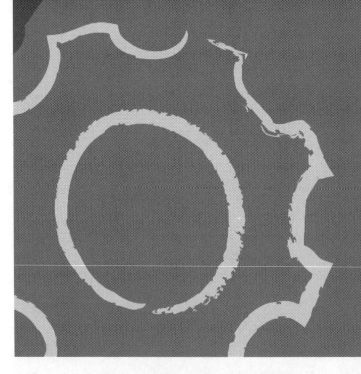

CHAPTER 16

People – How to Predict Behaviour

An increased understanding
of others leads to an
awareness of how people
are predictably different.

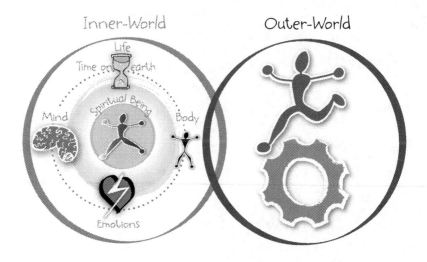

Your life revolves around people

If you look around you, you will see your Outer-World full of people; family, work colleagues, your boss, friends, neighbours and strangers. People are involved and present in every aspect of your life and are, therefore, an inevitable part of your life. As people occupy most of life, the ability to relate well to others would be very beneficial indeed!

You will certainly have noticed that people are different from each other. These differences may seem random and unpredictable. However, this is not so. People may be different, but they are predictably different.

Wouldn't it be great if you could predict what another person was going to do or how they would behave in certain situations? How about if you could predict the outcome of an interaction with someone before it even happened? It is very easy to understand how being able to predict your own or another person's behaviour could be both beneficial and powerful.

As the saying goes, knowledge is power. This is particularly true when it comes to knowledge about people. In fact, people knowledge leads to an increased understanding of others, which in turn leads to awareness of how people are predictably different. This awareness gives you more respect for people's differences as well as improving your ability to relate to others.

How to read people

Maya Angelou once said, "If someone shows you who they are, believe them." While this is a very simple statement, the message behind it is extremely important. Every day, the people around you reveal who they are in so many situations. The more interesting and challenging part however, is being able to understand what is revealed to you. To do that, you must be totally present and pay very close attention.

It is time now for you to become a "people scholar". By deliberately setting aside time to learn and understand other people, you will increase your knowledge, awareness of and respect for others, as well as your ability to relate to them.

How do people reveal themselves to you?

In your desire to read other people, there are four sources of information to be aware of:

1. How the person acts and behaves,
2. How the person looks (their appearance),
3. How the person relates to other people, and
4. How the person communicates.

As suggested above, people tend to act, behave, dress and communicate in very much a predetermined and predictable manner. So, even though every person around you is a distinctively different individual, knowledge of appropriate people-reading tools will empower you to understand them. These tools will help you evaluate, assess and make sense of the information revealed to you. They will allow you to categorise people's personalities and behaviours and enable you to better understand both yourself and other people.

The two most useful people prediction tools

There are many useful systems available for categorising and evaluating people's personalities and behaviour. However, the following two tools are particularly beneficial in assessing and gaining people knowledge. With a thorough understanding of these tools you will be able to predict the behaviour of yourself and others.

Your two people prediction tools are:

1. The Trisona System, and
2. The VAK System – Visual, Auditory and Kinaesthetic.

1. The Trisona System

What type of persona are you? Did you know that there are three major types of persona in the world and they explain the behaviour and personality of most people?

The three personas referred to are:

- The Loner,
- The Team Player, and
- The Talker.

By improving your observation skills and deliberately seeking to understand the personality traits associated with each of these personas, you will begin to recognise the differences between different people and increase your ability to accurately predict their behaviour.

As a Loner, YOU:
Think about work and everything that you have to do and want to do first
Always have a list of tasks and goals that you want to complete and accomplish
Feel that there are many dangers and threats lurking in your environment
Always see and focus on the risk, danger or potential harm in any situation first
Will always focus on what is wrong with something or what is not quite good enough. 99% might be perfect, but your attention will be drawn to the 1% flaw
Tend to be cautious in your approach
Tend to be pessimistic
Are somewhat prone to depression and tend to be negative in your attitude
Require a lot of information before making a decision
Are focussed on the detail
Have high standards - your work will be detailed and perfect / to a very high standard

Expect high standards of yourself and others
Buy the BEST of anything or at least the very best you can afford
Tend to be a perfectionist
Are very methodical, systematic and process driven in your approach
Want things to be orderly and neat
Are analytical - you like to analyse and compare detailed information
Evaluate yourself and others more on tasks than character
Procrastinate because you are unsure of what the BEST course of action is – paralysis by analysis
Are business-like and professional in your communication
Are tolerant and respectful of others, yet you feel uncomfortable around people and prefer to work alone
Dislike social gatherings, especially large crowds
Prefer small groups (no more than six people), if you must socialise
Always have a list of tasks that you must accomplish and you will prioritise doing the task above spending time with people
Tend to be more independent, solitary and self-contained
Follow the rules and get annoyed when other people bend or break the rules
Are an uncompromising worker
Tend to be a workaholic and must make a concerted effort not to spend all your time working
Are conscientious
Are creative and often artistic
Prefer everything in writing because that makes it "real" for you
Avoid conflict and confrontations with others as much as possible
Do a good job but always feel that you could and should have improved on your effort
Are never quite satisfied with your performance
Very seldom, if ever experience loneliness

As a Team Player, YOU:
Are people minded
Are people orientated
Think about people first
Look on the world as a reasonably safe place
Are friendly and social in your approach to others
Are pleasing, kind and caring
Are family oriented
Tend to be optimistic
Are communicative and enjoy speaking to and being with other people
Are a team player and enjoy doing things with other people
Are able to steadily work your way to complete tasks however you will take as much time as you have available to complete any task
Are casual and reserved
Tend to slow down and become passive-aggressive when you disagree with someone
Enjoy discussing other people – you talk about other people to others often
Are not completely clear about what you want from life or what you want to achieve; or you might have many things you want to achieve or do but are unable to decide on one to start on
Procrastinate because you are unsure exactly what you want
Live at a steady pace, slowing down when you feel pushed
Prefer that things stay the same and resist change
Want to be consulted and involved in decisions
Tend to hold a grudge
Enjoy storing things up and find it difficult to throw things away
Are agreeable and easy to get along with
Desire stability
Are reliable and amicable

Take it very personally and feel like the other person has questioned your character and integrity when you are criticised or questioned about a task

Will try to maintain balance in your life

Tend to keep your feelings inside and your opinions to yourself

As a Talker, YOU:
Are outgoing
LOVE TO TALK – especially about yourself and other people
Are very friendly
Are enthusiastic
Are trusting – you trust your environment and others readily
Are very social
Are open and approachable
Love to encourage others
Persuade others without trying – a natural sales person – even if you are only 'selling' your opinion
Enjoy being the centre of attention
Want to be popular and do popular things
Want to be friends with everybody
Laugh out loud – in fact you are loud
Enjoy being social and you love a party
Are optimistic and enthusiastic by nature
Want your work to be FUN
Are disorganised
Are spontaneous
Are opinionated
Dislike routine
Will openly display your emotions

Tend to be emotional
Will mention your weaknesses to others and openly discuss your short comings
Enjoy new things and new adventures
Often come up with new ideas
Tend to focus on the Big Picture and feel frustrated by detail
Tend to exaggerate
Have great people skills

Most people's personalities comprise of a combination of Team Player, Loner and Talker elements. The combination percentage will vary from person to person. However, people will tend to have a predominant persona with lesser influence from the other two elements.

What is the proportion of Loners, Team Players and Talkers in our society? Out of every 10 people you know, there will be:

- 1 Talker (10% of society),
- 2 Loners (20% of society), and
- 7 Team Players (70% of society).

How do you relate to people with the different personas?

Knowing your own persona and being able to decipher that of other people, will let you understand and respect the differences between you and focus on the strengths of their predominant character traits. With this knowledge you will effectively be able to adjust your interaction and communication with them which will in turn improve your relationships.

How do you relate to a Loner?

In your interaction with Loners:

DO:

- ✓ Communicate in a low key and professional manner.
- ✓ Be prepared to answer a lot of detailed questions about any topic that you are discussing.

    ✓   Give them a lot of information and be detailed in your communication.

    ✓   Take an interest in something that they are interested in.

DON'T:

    ✕   Talk about other people.

    ✕   Be over friendly or loud.

    ✕   Flatter them.

    ✕   Criticise them, especially on their tasks.

    ✕   Be pushy.

EXPECT a Loner to:

- Want to spend a lot of time alone.
- Ask detailed questions.
- Want a lot of information.
- Want to do things – sitting and talking is not an activity they enjoy.
- Try and avoid social functions.
- View facts as more important than relationships.
- View tasks as more important than people.
- Tend to be very good at their job.
- Not make quick decisions – they procrastinate and tend to get lost in the detail.
- Love anything that improves their standards or efficiency.

How do you relate to a Team Player:

In your interaction with a Team Player:

DO:

    ✓   Be their friend.

    ✓   Build rapport and trust.

    ✓   Be reserved.

    ✓   Be casual.

    ✓   Maintain plenty of eye contact during communication.

DON'T:

    ✕   Be pushy.

    ✕   Be rushed.

    ×   Introduce change.

    ×   Be loud and overly friendly.

EXPECT a Team Player to:
- ✓ Be steady in their decision making.
- ✓ Not make quick decisions.
- ✓ Slow down when feeling pressured.
- ✓ Live at a steady pace.
- ✓ Enjoy stability and predictability.
- ✓ Tend to be consistent.

How do you relate to a Talker?

In your interaction with a Talker:

DO:
- ✓ Be their friend.
- ✓ Be outgoing, friendly and loud.
- ✓ Flatter and compliment them.
- ✓ Have a sense of humour and laugh out loud.
- ✓ Show you care about them as a person.
- ✓ Be fun loving.
- ✓ Be chatty.
- ✓ Be sincere.

DON'T:
- × Be boring.
- × Bore them with a lot of detail.
- × Reject them.
- × Make them feel you would rather do a task than spend time with them.

EXPECT a Talker to:
- Be fun loving.
- Be positive and outgoing.
- Not be good at administration.
- Be quite disorganised.
- Have great people skills.
- Be friendly.
- Not handle rejection well.
- Be overly emotional.

2. The VAK System

The second extremely valuable tool to help you understand what "makes people tick" and relate better to other people, is known as VAK.

So what is VAK? VAK is an acronym for Visual, Auditory and Kinaesthetic as described in NLP by Richard Bandler and John Grinder. As discussed in Chapter 4 on Perception, you rely on your five senses to gather information from your environment. More than that, those senses form your point of contact for interaction with the environment and therefore they heavily influence how you live.

Your senses are seeing, hearing, tasting, smelling and feeling, with most information being received into your brain by seeing it, hearing it or feeling it. Even though people use all of their senses, each person has an innate preference for one sense on which they rely most.
So:

- If you prefer to rely on your sight you will be known as Visual,
- If you prefer to rely on your hearing you will be known as Auditory, and
- If you prefer to rely on your touch and bodily feeling, you will be known as Kinaesthetic.

Therefore, VAK describes the sense preference that each person has for receiving information and interacting with their environment.

What does this mean for you?

By gaining a working knowledge of this tool you will further improve your understanding of other people and your ability to relate and build rapport with others.

Visual People
Rely mostly on their eyes to gather most information from their environment.
Create and see pictures in their mind.
Are very good at visualising in their mind.
Have difficulty comprehending long conversations and a lot of verbal information.

Visual People

Include in their vocabulary many words of a visual nature like: see, look, picture, clear, reveal and focus.
Are particularly interested in how things look – appearance is VERY important to them.
Are easily distracted by movement around them.
Stand or sit with their heads and bodies erect.
Are neat, well groomed and orderly.
Organise the space in front of them neatly.
Sit in a neat / precise manner.
Perform deliberate actions.
Memorise by seeing images in their mind.
Are not distracted by noise.
Quite often are very good at spelling.
Have difficulty remembering long oral instructions and explanations – their mind will tend to wander.
Respond well to highly descriptive language.
Have the ability to memorise many things at one time.

Auditory People

Rely mostly on their sense of hearing.
Learn, receive messages and memorise through the act of listening to auditory stimuli such as speech, music, radio, etc.
Are distracted by noise.
Like to receive verbal instructions.
Include in their vocabulary auditory words/phrases like: That sounds good; Let's talk; Did you hear that; It's been great talking to you; Manner of speaking; Word for word; Listen; Hear.
Sit relaxed in their chair.
Tilt their heads to one side slightly when listening.
Tend to be of medium build.

Auditory People

Can be well dressed but are just as likely to be casually dressed.

Renowned for talking to themselves.

Are easily distracted by noise or sound.

Memorise predominantly through their auditory senses and this means they absorb information sequentially because they can only hear one sound at a time.

Will be able to recall conversations verbatim – even conversations you had with them a year ago.

Respond well to carefully chosen words and to changes in tonality.

Will immediately notice if you are remotely tired, bored or uninterested, or if your attention has lapsed while talking to them.

Kinaesthetic People

Rely predominantly on their sense of feeling.

Are particularly interested that things in their environment feel right.

Respond to physical touch.

Prefer to experience and do something as opposed to looking at it (Visual person) or speaking about it (Auditory person).

Tend to stand closer to people.

Memorise by doing, walking through something or experiencing it.

Speak very slowly.

Dress comfortably.

Include in their vocabulary words/phrases that are kinaesthetic in nature like: feel; touch; grab; grasp; make contact; concrete; I can't get a handle on that; We better get in touch with; Hold onto that idea; Let me step you through this; Come to grips with; Get hold of.

Tend to be heavily built or heavier boned.

Are very relaxed physically and could lean back or drape themselves over a chair.

Typically talk in a very slow manner, pronouncing words individually one after the other because they are trying to get a feel for how things are, according to them. Feelings take much longer to process than sounds or pictures.

Kinaesthetic People
Should not be underestimated regarding intelligence despite their slowness of speech or the slower pace at which they process information.
Constantly pass information received over their feelings, which takes time.
Respond to physical rewards like a pat on the back.
Are "touchy-feely" people.
Are physical in their nature.
Want to experience things and really enjoy physical contact.
Will quickly notice if you wince or withdraw when they touch you.

What is the proportion of Visual, Auditory and Kinaesthetic people in society? Out of every 10 people you know, there will be:

- 4 Visual people (40% of population).

- 2 Auditory people (20% of population).

- 4 Kinaesthetic people (40% of population).

People Mastery

Once you have mastered the Trisona and VAK systems, the next step is to pay attention to the dynamic interaction that each of the two different systems can have in one person.

The following two examples explain this interaction:
- A **visual loner** person will be focussed on detail as well as very concerned with the appearance of both themselves and the things around them. This interaction gives us someone who is ALWAYS perfectly dressed and presented and who will always look after their possessions very well. Their work will always be of a high standard, very neat and well presented. Their environment, their desk, their car, etc. will always be neat, tidy and look good.

- A **kinaesthetic loner** will also focus on the detail. However, they will be comfortably dressed and might even look sloppy. Their desk and environment will be comfortable and might also appear messy. Their communication style will be very slow. Their work will be of a high standard but not necessarily well presented.

Similar interaction of traits is present for every combination of persona and VAK element. Logically therefore, this creates numerous combinations of behaviour, appearance, communication style and interaction with others. Mastering these systems and understanding their interacting elements will make predicting and understanding yours and other people's behaviour straight forward and easy to identify and use.

Living an extraordinary life involves having an ability to get along with other people, to relate successfully to them and to maintain happy relationships with some of them.

By arming yourself with the above tools and information you will greatly improve your awareness and understanding of other people. This in turn will foster in you, a greater sense of appreciation and respect for people's differences. It will allow you to be kind and flexible in your interactions with others and create happy relationships for a happy life!

CHAPTER 17

Be The Best You

What in your opinion makes a person worthy? Is it your career? Your address? The title on your business card? Your bank balance? Have you achieved an acceptable level of worthiness yet? Will you ever feel worthy?

Take a moment to imagine a child in a remote village in Africa. Picture this child who is growing up in extreme poverty with tattered clothes, a dirty face, no shoes and big dark eyes, playing in the dust in front of a makeshift shelter. Do you have a mental image of that child?

Is this child worthy? The answer is a resounding YES! Yet, that child is unlikely to ever achieve what is defined as greatness by western culture. That child is unlikely to have the right address, wear the right clothing, attend the best schools, or have a bank balance. Yet, this child is worthy!

Worthiness is not achieved, nor is it earned. Worthiness is granted to YOU by virtue of your mere existence. There is nothing you can be, do or have that will make you any more or less worthy. Appreciate the worthiness of those around you. Recognise just how profoundly worthy you are and believe it!

We are all similar and equal

As human beings, we share many similarities! In fact, as a human race, we share more commonalities than differences. We all share the need for health, food and clean air to breathe; we all desire safety for our families and opportunities for our kids. We share a deep desire to love and be loved; we want our lives to be significant. We all want to work to our strengths and do what we love; we all have an innate desire to contribute, to know God and to live extraordinarily.

You are unique!

While we share many similarities, there is nobody exactly like YOU! No one thinks exactly like you, lives the same life as you or loves the same way you do. The only one who is like you – is you!

For this reason, no one can impact this world exactly like you. No one else can make quite the same contribution as you can. You were created for a reason! It is up to you to fill the void that exists in the world that you were meant to fill. You and your life are important, but it is up to YOU to make it count.

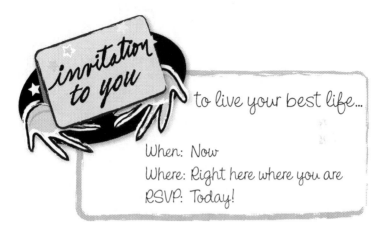

Invitation

I would like to extend an invitation to you to live your best and extraordinary life. What do I mean by this? I want you to know that you have control of your life and, with this control, you have the ability to determine the quality of the life you live. No one else lives your life but you and it is only you who has the power to create the life you wish to live.

Here's a visual exercise for you. Find somewhere comfortable to sit; it could be in your favourite chair or while you are lying down reading this book. Now, imagine you are in a large room full of shelves and on those shelves are boxes. You have been asked to choose just one box, but there are so many to choose from; there are big boxes and small boxes, and all are wrapped differently. Some are brightly wrapped; some have big bows, while others sparkle in the light; but out of all of these hundreds of boxes, you have to choose just one.

You know this one box is special; it holds promises that all the other boxes do not have; it is the "ultimate prize" and it is just for you. This box contains your "extraordinary life", not some ordinary life but the life the powerful YOU could possibly live. All of the other boxes contain different versions of your life, but none of them will have the same splendour of your "extraordinary life".

Wander around these boxes; look at them, study their shape, their colour and take the time to find the one that is right for you. Choose wisely. Once you have chosen your box, study it, and feel it and examine the emotions it evokes.

Now, I encourage you to open the box - make it yours. This is your life; it is the best life there could ever be for you and only you. Embrace it. Love it. Choose to live an extraordinary life now! This choice is available to you now and in every moment of every day.

Did you notice there were two actions you needed to do to complete this exercise?

One – you needed to choose the best box for you.

And…

Two – you had to take possession of the box. You needed to own it, control it and make it yours in every sense.

You deserve to live your best and extraordinary life! Now, go for it!

In the end…

In the end the Naked Truth will prevail. Creating your own unique extraordinary life starts with taking charge of your Inner-world. Allow YOU as a spiritual being to master, use and control your mind, your body and your emotions. Enjoy your time on earth. Stop living a life of mere coincidence and take charge of your destiny! The life you have always wanted awaits you…

Quick reference guide

1. **How do you reprogram your subconscious mind?**
   Please refer to chapter 5 page 46.

2. **How do you change your negative thinking-feeling patterns?**
   Please refer to chapter 6 page 65.

3. **How can you feel good?**
   Please refer to chapter 7 page 74.

4. **How can you cope with unpleasant emotions?**
   Please refer to chapter 8 page 89.

5. **How can you smash your shackles and forgive?**
   Please refer to chapter 9 page 109.

6. **How can you take care of your body?**
   Please refer to chapter 10 page 114.

7. **How can you create an extraordinary life?**
   Please refer to chapter 11 page 132.

8. **How can you create an ideal routine?**
   Please refer to chapter 12 page 142.

9. **How can you discover your Life's Work?**
   You possess many talents, gifts, strengths and abilities, but the responsibility falls to you to discover, develop, and contribute your talents, gifts, strengths and abilities to those around you.

   The clues to your Life's Work are found in you.

   Please go to www.nakedtruthaboutyou.com for a detailed step-by-step process you can follow to discover your Life's Work. If you are already engaged in your Life's Work, go to www.nakedtruthaboutyou.com/statement for instructions and examples on how to write your Life's Work Statement.

As soon as you have defined what your Life's Work entails, take full responsibility for its completion. Remember, if you do not engage with your Life's Work and meet the need that exists in the world, your work will sadly remain undone. Only you have the ability to fulfil your Life's Work.

10. **How can you solve a problem?**
    Please refer to chapter 14 page 165.

11. **How can you be a solution finder?**
    Please refer to chapter 14 page 168.

12. **How can you set goals?**
    Please refer to chapter 14 page 171.

13. **How can you make other's opinions of you count?**
    Please refer to chapter 14 page 174.

14. **How can you ultimately overcome problems, achieve goals, and get the most out of other people's opinions of you?**
    Please refer to chapter 14 page 175.

15. **How can you predict people's behaviour?**
    Please refer to chapter 16 page 185.

Biography

With a background in psychology and business, Elize Hattin is a coach of rare quality, who successfully helps clients to achieve significant success in their lives, professions and businesses.

She has worked as an international life and business coach, executive consultant and business facilitator in Australia, the United Kingdom, South Africa and Europe. Her client base is broad and she has coached business owners, corporate clients, business executives, managers, advertising executives, academics, young professionals and students to improved performance, results and quality of life.

Elize was born and raised in South Africa where she met and married her husband Wald. As a young couple desperate for adventure and new experiences, they moved to London where their first child was born. After some years in England they chose to relocate to Australia, where they now reside happily with their two daughters.

Elize is passionate about helping people develop and succeed. This passion forms the cornerstone of her Life's Work. Her driven yet caring nature is a great asset to her clients, assisting them in achieving their best.

Elize is the founder and director of Influence Global. Elize and her team provide quality executive, business and life coaching.

Elize is also a popular public speaker; entertaining, informing and inspiring her audiences.

Elize is living her dream of assisting as many as possible to reach their life potential, achieve success and live happy, wealthy lives. This book is but one more step towards realising that dream.

Bibliography

Access Economics (2004). Wake Up Australia: The Value of Healthy Sleep, Report to Sleep Health Australia.

Bob Proctor: http://bobproctor.com

Brown, D.J.W. (2005). Insomnia Prevalence and Daytime Consequences, In T. Lee-Chiong (Ed.), *Sleep: A Comprehensive Handbook* (pp. 91-98). Hoboken: John Wiley & Sons, Inc.

Chiropractors' Association of Australia,
http://chiropractors.asn.au/AM/Template.cfm?Section=Sleep&Template=/CM/ContentDisplay.cfm&ContentID=1867

Covey, S.R. (1989). *The 7 Habits of Highly Effective People*, Free Press.

Davis, D. & Clifton A. (1995). Psychosocial Theory: Erikson. Retrieved from http://www.haverford.edu/psych/ddavis/p109g/erikson.stages.html

Frankl, V.E. (1959). *Man's search for meaning.* Beacon Press.

Listverse Fact & Fiction. Top 15 Amazing Facts About the Human Body. Retrieved from http://listverse.com/2008/06/10/top-15-amazing-facts-about-the-human-body/

Maxwell, J.C. (2008) *Make today count: The Secret of your Success is Determined by your Daily Agenda,* Hachette Book Group.

Meyer, B.J., Van Papendorp, D.H., Meij, H.S., & Viljoen, M. (2002). *Human Physiology.* Juta.

The National Sleep Research Project – 40 amazing facts about sleep. (2000), retrieved from http://www.abc.net.au/science/sleep/facts.htm

O'Connor, J. & McDermott, I. (1996). *Way of NLP.* Thorsons.

Shakespeare, W. *As you like it.*

Researchers say lack of sleep doubles risk of death...but so can too much sleep. (2007). Retrieved from http://www2.warwick.ac.uk/newsandevents/press-releases/researchers_say_lack/

Winter (1987). Leadership Vol.8, No.1

World Bank: www.worldbank.org

Contact details

Email Elize at:
elize@elizehattin.com

For general enquiries:
office@elizehattin.com

For coaching:
coach@elizehattin.com

www.elizehattin.com

Join the movement of people all over the world who are coming together to learn more about themselves and how to influence the world, by searching:
Elize Hattin Coaching Group on Facebook

Do you have friends that are not living their own unique extraordiary life. Please recommend this book to them.

Look out for more great books by the author.

Coaches Training

Do YOU have a PASSION for PEOPLE and want to change the world?

We will assist you to

✓ Draw on your Inner Passions and Soul Purpose to Create a Better World

✓ Become the Best You can Be by Influencing Others to be the Best They can Be

Contact us at

Influence Global
Training

For more information on training, please visit our website

www.influenceglobal.com   office@influenceglobal.com

Corporate Coaching and Training

Are YOU a top performing EXECUTIVE who wants to improve your personal performance as well as the performance of your Organisation?

We will assist you to

✓ Go from Inner Influence to Local Influence to a Simple Formula for Global Influence

✓ Create Relentless Purpose, Collective Missions, Loyalty-Producing Culture and Control through Predictable Planning

Contact us at

Influence Global
Executive

www.influenceglobal.com   office@influenceglobal.com

Life Coaching and Training

Do you want to create the life of your dreams?

We will assist you to

- ✓ Overcome the Disappointments of your Current Life
- ✓ Make the Rest of your Life the Best of your Life
- ✓ Find your Life Purpose and Achieve it
- ✓ Become a Person of Influence

Contact us at

Influence Global
Life

www.influenceglobal.com   office@influenceglobal.com

Business Coaching and Training

Are you a business owner or business manager who wants to improve the performance of your business without sacrificing your life in the process?

We will assist you to create a

- ✓ Disciplined Team
- ✓ Loyalty Producing Clarity
- ✓ Hands-Off Systems
- ✓ Sustainable Consistency
- ✓ Never-Fail Profit Drivers

Contact us at

Influence Global
Business

www.influenceglobal.com   office@influenceglobal.com